More than Champions

Mario Andretti
Dave Dravecky
Cathy Rigby
and others

DIMENSIONS

FOR LIVING

NASHVILLE

MORE THAN CHAMPIONS

This book is printed on recycled, acid-free paper.

Library of Congress Cataloging-in-Publication Data

ANDRETTI, MARIO, 1940-
    More than champions / Mario Andretti, Dave Dravecky, Cathy Rigby, and others.
        p.   cm.
    ISBN 0-687-27191-6 (alk. paper)
    1. Athletes—Religious life—Case studies.   I. Dravecky, Dave.   II. Rigby, Cathy, 1952-   .   III. Title.
    BV4596.A8A53   1992
    248.8'8—dc20   92-2814
                                                                                          CIP

Scripture quotations marked KJV are from the King James Version of the Bible.

Those marked RSV are from the Revised Standard Version of the Bible copyright 1946, 1952, 1971 by the Division of Christian Education of the National Council of Churches of Christ in the USA. Used by permission.

Those marked NIV are taken from the *Holy Bible: New International Version*. Copyright © 1973, 1978, 1984 by the International Bible Society. Used by permission of Zondervan Bible Publishers.

MANUFACTURED IN THE UNITED STATES OF AMERICA

Contents

And Then Some

Hank Aaron

Back in the fifties, as a young baseball player with the Milwaukee Braves, the last thing I ever imagined was my ending up in the Hall of Fame. Baseball swarms with hopeful rookies, but only a handful make a name and a career in the majors. I was young and talented. But so were a lot of other players. I had a great dream and worked hard, doing what was expected of me. But so did lots of others. I wasn't sure I had it in me to go all the way. *What does it take?* I wondered.

During that time my wife gave birth to twins. Tragically, one of them was just too small and sick. He was dying. That's when a young priest came into my life. When Father Seblica arrived in our hospital room, I could tell there was something different about him. We'd never met before, we weren't even Catholic, but he sat with us longer than he had to, expressing an extra measure of concern.

After that we became friends. He taught me to play handball. And even though I was younger and an athlete, he often beat me. He ran after the ball the way he had reached out to bereaved parents—he gave it something extra.

Then one day I ran into problems getting my child accepted at a private school. Father Seblica responded with his special vigor, talking to school officials, writing letters and taking a stand.

"What is it with you, Father?" I asked when he told me he was making progress.

"Oh, I do what I can," he answered. *"And then some."*

And then some. That was the secret that made his life extraordinary. And that's the way I began to play baseball: not only doing what was expected of me, but trying to give something extra beyond what was required. I found it took more than talent to keep smashing the ball out of the park, or to make an "impossible" catch. It took an undefinable extra dimension of self-giving.

Things started happening in my career. I began to make All-Star teams and lead the league in hitting. Before I knew it, I was breaking Babe Ruth's all-time homerun mark of 714.

Today, I'm helping to develop the Atlanta Braves' minor-league teams. And sometimes I look at the eager faces and abundance of talent, and I see myself all over again—a kid looking for a way to be all I could be. I try to show them that whatever you're striving for, in sports or any other endeavor, Father Seblica's approach to life holds the key: doing what you can . . . *and then some.*

 # The Loving Voice of God
Lionel Aldridge

One of the most frightening signs that there was something seriously wrong with me were the voices I began hearing in 1974. At first they were just stray, nagging worries that dogged me through the day, self-doubts that we all have from time to time. They seemed to rise up out of nowhere—vague thoughts with an accusing edge: *You really don't work very hard, do you?* Or I'd be alone in my car and it was as if I overheard someone whisper, *Everyone knows Lionel Aldridge doesn't care about his job.*

The fact was I worked hard and cared very much about my job. I was something of a fixture on the Milwaukee scene. After an all-pro career as a defensive end with coach Vince Lombardi's two-time Super Bowl champion Green Bay Packers football team, I'd moved easily into the role of NFL commentator and local TV sports anchor. I had a successful, high-profile life.

That was before the voices.

The voices were very scary and confusing. I didn't know what to do. I didn't want anyone to find out the terrible things happening inside my head. As an athlete I'd been trained to be tough; it was not my nature to seek help. I wanted to be strong.

At first I tried to ignore them. I was just going through a bad period, I thought. But the voices grew more belittling and threatening, more real. I'd be standing in front of the mirror shaving when I'd hear from the next room, *You don't take very good care of your family.* "That's bull!" I'd shout. I'd search the house for my tormentor. "How'd he get in here?" I'd mutter, as my wife, Viki, shook her head in dismay. There never was any intruder.

If a co-worker at the station didn't smile at me in the morning, a voice would hiss, *See? He doesn't think much of you either. He knows you don't deserve your job.* I became hard to get along with. I started talking back to the voices, bickering and pleading and cursing. I am a large and imposing man; it must have scared folks half out of their wits to see me shouting at people who weren't there.

Rumors flew around town that I was on drugs. That was completely false, but I was in no shape to prove otherwise. I was getting worse. People wanted to help but they didn't know how. "He's under a lot of pressure," I heard them say.

One night, attending a Bucks basketball game with a friend, I froze with terror as we moved in front of the crowd toward our courtside VIP seats.

"What's wrong?" my friend asked.

"These people," I stammered, "they . . . they know everything I'm thinking. They're all watching me."

I was dizzy with panic. I wanted to run.

"Take it easy," my puzzled friend whispered, looking at me as if he suspected I was playing a gag on him. Then he saw the perspiration drenching my shirt collar. "Maybe you're working too hard," he muttered, putting an arm on my shoulder and easing me into my seat.

Soon that feeling of being watched wouldn't let up, even on the air. Looking into the camera, I could barely hold my composure as I reported the nightly sports scores. The wide camera lens zooming in on me was a glistening, all-seeing eye that could plumb the farthest, most hidden reaches of my soul. Everyone who was watching on their TV sets, I was convinced, could see right inside my brain, where laid bare for all to look on in disgust were the grimmest secrets of my life.

I was sure there was a far-flung conspiracy to destroy me. I fought with total strangers on the street. I separated from Viki and our two daughters, and eventually divorced. I lost my job and my friends. There was nothing left but the voices shouting in my head, as real to me as an opposing 260-pound pulling guard on a goal-line stand back in my playing days. My life spun out of control.

One night the voices commanded me to start driving. I didn't want to leave Milwaukee. It had been my home for so many good years, and a part of me still understood that I needed a home now more than ever. But my state of extreme delusion robbed me of choice.

I hastily packed up the car with some old clothes and a few basics. Almost as an afterthought I threw in a Bible I'd owned since the Packers. I used to take it with me when I traveled with the team. Even now I'd read it to try and drown out the voices. What little relief I could get sometimes came from immersing myself in that old Bible.

I started to drive with no map or plan—I just filled up on gas and went. I tried to turn back; I couldn't do it.

I crisscrossed the country in a wilderness of interstates. At first I slept in hotels, then motels, then flophouses. I went to Chicago, Kansas City, Dallas, Sacramento, Las Vegas. My funds evaporated and my credit cards were cancelled, so I started living in the car, occasionally washing dishes for food and gas. In Florida I ditched the car for a hundred dollars and hit the streets with just a battered satchel on my shoulder.

Occasionally I hung around a town for a while doing odd jobs, living on the streets and eating at soup kitchens. Quite naturally, people would stare at me, and that would only make my delusions of persecution worse. I never held a job for long. What could you do about a menial laborer who marched and sang for no reason and jabbered at people who were 2,000 miles away? Had I seen such a man on the street in Milwaukee only a few years before, I would have shook my head sadly and crossed to the other side.

I'd become one of those lost, devastated souls. There were a lot of them out there with me, crippled by mental illness, but as I wandered the country I was only aware of my own haunted, unhappy world a million miles from the life I once had.

One night I slept in a field off an interstate near the Great Salt Lake. I didn't notice when I woke up, but while I was sleeping my jewel-encrusted Super Bowl ring must have slipped off. Those rings are not easy to come by, and I'd hung on to mine as a kind of symbol of who I'd once been. No one ever questioned me about it. I guess they thought it was just some crazy piece of jewelry that a crazy man wore.

I didn't think about the Packers much anymore, and when I discovered the ring missing, it was as if I'd been stripped of one final link with my past. I sat in the middle of a sidewalk and wept into my hands.

It wasn't long afterward that I was gripped by a gruesome hallucination. I was hanging on a cross, like Jesus. Standing in a roadside ditch under a hot white cloudless Utah sky, legs together and arms outstretched, I vividly experienced my own crucifixion. It is hard to explain now, but in my tortured imagination I actually believed that I was living out the event. It seemed so absolutely real.

I remained that way for hours. People shouted from cars whizzing by on the desert highway. A few threw objects at me. But I was anchored to that spot, fully convinced that I could be seen hanging on a cross and no one cared.

"Help me!" I cried out, the sweat and tears streaking my dust-caked face. "Help! I'll accept help from anyone."

That night, exhausted and hungry, I huddled beside a bridge and read my battered Bible, the only thing left now from my old life. I still had moments when I could dimly perceive reality. A core part of me knew that I must get well. But that clarity was fleeting, and my madness always took me back in circles and filled me with hurt and fear.

I was reading Paul when I came across a passage that stopped me: "Earnestly seek the higher gifts." I'd been taught that these gifts were spiritual, given by God to lift us up. Were they still there for me? I wondered what gift could be found in the demented chorus that chased me across the country. Those voices were so angry and critical.

Yet didn't I know all along that there was one voice with me my whole life, a flowing, wordless voice that said, *You are loved?* It was the voice of God, a voice for all of us to hear in our own way. I'd never stopped believing in God, but His voice had been drowned out by my illness. When I stopped long enough to listen, I knew that with God I had hope, I had love. That was what Paul was talking about.

Eventually I wandered back to Milwaukee. The voices still besieged me. I lived on the streets. Being back brought me in contact with old friends. I was ashamed for them to see what I'd come to. I tried to hide. Yet for some reason I'd come back here. I knew that.

Finally, through the repeated intervention of people I'd known for a long time, I was committed to a hospital. I didn't want to go in—I thought it was all part of the big conspiracy. Commitment is difficult legally, and I made it harder. Yet it marked the start of the road back.

I learned that I had paranoid schizophrenia, a physical disease that affects the mind. Hearing voices was one of the symptoms. Slowly the doctors hit upon some drugs that helped. Little by little my condition improved, the voices gradually subsided.

At first it was horrifying. It was an awful thing to face, like seeing a crazy man on the street and suddenly realizing that you are looking into a mirror. One day during therapy, I begged the doctor to show me one person who'd recovered from paranoid schizophrenia.

"Well, Lionel," he replied, "statistically many people do recover partially, even fully." He went to quote all the facts and figures.

"No," I interrupted, "I want to actually *meet* someone who's beat it."

There was no one to show me. People who recover from mental illness rarely divulge that devastating stigma. It would have helped me to see someone who'd come back. "If I get out of here, Doc," I promised him. "I'm going to make a point of talking about it."

I *did* recover. Not without setbacks and relapses, not without moments when I thought I could never again face life, but I did get well with the help of friends, doctors who found the right medication to help me and the voice of a loving God.

I discovered new strategies to cope with the world. For a while, symptoms sometimes came back. Like one night after I got out of the hospital. I was walking up to a café near my apartment for dinner when suddenly I knew that every patron inside was saying terrible things about me. I stood at the door, terrified, my heart pounding. I was about to run home and lock myself in when I thought, *No, you've got to do this. You've got to go inside and face these people.*

Still I was convinced they were all talking about me. *Well,* I figured, *maybe they're saying good things like, "Hey, there's Lionel Aldridge. He used to play for the Packers and then he got sick. Look how good he's doing now."* If people really were saying bad things about me, I would have to forgive them. Forgiveness made what they said harmless; it didn't matter whether it was real or imagined.

I went inside, sat down and ordered my dinner. The room was alive with chatter. I was almost too nervous to eat. Then slowly it dawned on me that these people were talking about everything in the world *except* me.

It worked. From then on when I thought strangers were talking about me, I always convinced myself that they were saying good things or forgave them for the bad things I imagined them saying. And through the whole process I never stopped asking God's help or listening for His voice.

In time the voices went away. I still see a doctor and take my medication, like anyone with a serious illness, but I am well again, well enough to keep a promise. Today I travel the country speaking to groups about mental illness and recovery. It's vital for patients, families and even doctors to see someone who's actually made it back.

In January 1985, the anniversary of the Packers' first Super Bowl win 18 years before, I got a card in the mail from a bunch of my old teammates. They'd gotten together and commissioned an exact copy of the missing victory ring to give to me.

I knew that day that I had returned. Even when you think you've lost everything in your life, there is always hope of finding a way back, sometimes to an even better place.

I found my way, with the loving voice of God to guide me.

 # Yield unto Others

Mario Andretti

I was standing in one of those long lines leading up to the airline ticket counter. There weren't enough check-in clerks that morning. As I waited with other disgruntled travelers, a distraught man rushed up, glancing wildly at the clock and staring hopelessly at the line. It was obvious he was about to miss his plane.

Then something happened that changed the whole atmosphere. The man at the head of the line waved the harried latecomer on ahead of him. That little act of courtesy sent a ripple of kindness through us all. The tension lessened, faces relaxed.

But the pleasant feeling evaporated after I reached my destination. I was in a rental car on an expressway, in a crowd of other hurrying vehicles. Drivers cut in front of one another, horns blared, there were angry gestures.

I couldn't help thinking how strange it was that I would rather be hurtling along at 200 mph on the Indianapolis Speedway than driving at 55 mph on this expressway. Frankly, I'll take the Monaco Grand Prix, with its serpentine twists and turns, over a public highway any day. For I feel safer on the racecourse than I do on the streets.

And I have two very good reasons—one obvious and one not so obvious.

First, professional race-car drivers have their minds on driving when they're behind the wheel. Second, unlike too many motorists today, professional race-car drivers are exceedingly courteous to one another on the track.

To those of you who have watched the flat-out competition of an Indy car race or Grand Prix, that may sound hard to believe. But it's true. Spectators are not aware of the extraordinary amount of "please," "thank you" and "you're welcome" that goes on in a typical race. Most of it is done with hand signals.

This kind of courtesy is not required. There's nothing about it in the rule book. It even transcends sportsmanship. We race-car drivers are courteous to one another for a very simple reason—it saves lives. In my 30 years of racing, my own life has been spared by the thoughtfulness of fellow drivers more times than I care to recall.

One time, I think it was in 1976 at the Michigan International Speedway, A. J. Foyt did something that I'll never forget. Now, anyone who follows racing knows that A. J. and I are not exactly good buddies. We have a long-standing rivalry and we both strive all-out to win.

Halfway through the 500-mile race in Michigan we were all bunched up under a yellow caution light, traveling slow and holding our positions. I was near the head of the pack. A. J. was right behind me, waiting to leap ahead the instant the "all clear" green light flashed on. I was determined not to let him pass.

Next thing I knew, A. J. had pulled up alongside me, pointing to my rear axle and shaking his head no. I knew that if A. J. said something was wrong, something *was* wrong. So I pulled off the course. It wasn't until I was safe in the pits that I saw why he had warned me. A. J. had seen sparks shooting from the back of my racer, but there was no way I could have known that my half shaft, the rear axle, was about to fail.

Breaking a half shaft can be disastrous, for the car will usually careen to the right, and in the middle of a pack of racers, that could cause a pileup. A. J. could have sped along and done nothing. Indeed, it would have been to his advantage if I'd broken down and taken some of his other competitors with me. But A. J. is a pro who averted a disaster by his act of courtesy.

This sort of thing goes on all the time. We drivers are constantly trying to keep one another out of trouble.

For example, if a driver sees debris, spilled oil or an accident ahead, he'll raise a clenched fist to warn those behind him. At the speeds we travel it's our only hope of avoiding a rear-end collision.

Another example is passing. When a faster car is about to overtake another, the slower driver will point to the safer side to pass. Of course, nobody likes being passed, but the slower driver knows that a car passing on the wrong wide can spell trouble for both of them.

Then there's lane changing. Before a driver moves across the track to pull off into the pits, he carefully signals his intention. Letting the other driver know your plan helps both drivers.

It's not always the same on the public highway, where most of the hand signals I see these days are obscene. Even so, I try to bring my driving habits from the track to the highway. When I see someone's door ajar, or a low tire, or water leaking from a radiator, I warn him. When I see a dangerous situation ahead, such as a stalled truck, a stray animal or debris on the road, I tap my break pedal several times or turn on my flashers to warn those behind me. Before moving from lane to lane, I alert others by using my turn signal.

What I can't understand is why race-car drivers (strapped inside a tiny cockpit, steering, breaking, double-clutching, checking rearview mirrors, watching gauges—all at nearly 200 mph) have the time for these courtesies, while motorists tooling along in air-conditioned sedans often do not.

If motorists were half as courteous to one another as race-car drivers are, I think it would save thousands of lives. Unfortunately, somewhere along the line, courtesy has become confused with weakness. And that's a shame, because there's nothing wimpy about watching out for the other guy. Just ask Emerson Fittipaldi, Rick Mears, Danny Sullivan, Bobby Rahal—among the greatest of today's race drivers. They'll tell you courtesy is just plain good sense.

I remember during the German Grand Prix at Nürburgring racetrack when I battled for position with Niki Lauda, three-time world Grand Prix champion. Deep in the Black Forest, Niki and I were roaring down a steep hill with a sharp right turn at the bottom. I figured the turn was my only chance to pass him. One rule of thumb in racing is that the car in front follows what we call the line, the most direct route. Therefore the challenger must get around the leader by using the least advantageous part of the road.

Halfway down the hill I decided to pass Niki in a "banzai charge." If I waited until the last second to brake, with luck I might gain a slight lead.

Well, I'm not entirely sure what happened, but I found myself short, inside and behind Niki. Worse, he was about to "close the door" (legally cut me off), and I'd be forced off the road, into the woods. As it turned out, Niki saw the mess I was in. He made room for me so that I could stay on the course. Once again I was saved by another driver's courtesy.

A few weeks later we were driving in the Swedish Grand Prix, and Niki and I found ourselves in a similar situation; this time I was in the lead and Niki was charging from behind. I could have closed the door on Niki and sent him flying into the woods. But I made room for him instead. I hadn't forgotten the good turn he had done me.

It's reassuring when you can see this same give-and-take on the public highway. I was in a line of cars in town the other day, waiting at a red light. A light-blue sedan edged out from a shopping-center drive, obviously hoping to enter the line. I expected no one to give way. But the driver in front of me motioned for the blue sedan to move into the line. I had occasion to follow the light-blue sedan for a few miles and saw him do the same thing for others.

One act of courtesy invites another. Unfortunately, the reverse is true. When a driver is cut off, even if he senses the move was not done deliberately, he often gets angry, and anger can lead to all kinds of irrational—and dangerous—behavior.

When two strangers accidentally brush each other on a sidewalk, usually there are apologies and smiles. But put these same two people in their cars and they become totally different. Somehow automobiles seem to harden us. We stop thinking about the other driver; we think only of ourselves.

There's an old Italian proverb, *Beretta in mano non fece mai danno*, which means "Cap in hand never did anyone harm." It's true. Humility has a lot to do with courtesy. Getting outside yourself, being considerate, making those small sacrifices—courtesy is thinking of others first.

Something to remember when you and I are out on the highways—and on the highway of life.

 # Not on My Own

Rocky Bleier

"What did you do in civilian life, son?" the Army doctor in Tokyo asked me, after he'd finished examining the bandages on both my legs.

"I was drafted by the Pittsburgh Steelers as a running back, before the Army drafted me," I said bitterly.

The doctor's eyes searched mine.

"Well," he said gently, "your football days are over. Thank God you're not permanently crippled."

I wasn't thankful. I was mad. And I was scared. Not of the pain— I was used to punishing my body. I was afraid of being a "gimp."

And I wouldn't accept the doctor's diagnosis. I was determined to make my legs run again.

Back in Vietnam, my platoon had been attacked by a large force of North Vietnamese. We were cut off. Close-quarters fighting. I was hit in the left thigh by small-arms fire. I went down. Collapsed even before I felt the pain. "God, no," I pleaded. "Not my leg." Then a grenade exploded right at my feet. Shrapnel tore into both legs, shattering bones in my right foot.

I started crawling toward cover, dragging my legs. *I can make it,* I thought. Then I started to pass out. At that moment a black soldier I'd never seen before came and picked me up. Under fire, he wrapped my arms around his neck and lifted. Then, carrying me on his back, he started to the rear. Two miles away there was a landing spot for evacuation helicopters.

He carried me a mile and then collapsed. But stretcher bearers found me and got me to the choppers. I never knew his name, but I'll never forget him. When I could do nothing for myself, God sent him. He saved my life.

The war was over for me. They patched me up and sent me back to the States. Eventually, I found myself in Fort Riley, Kansas, waiting to be discharged. It was July, 1970. I was an out-of-work rookie football player with a 40 percent disability rating from the Army. But I was too stubborn to accept the doctor's verdict. I intended to try out for the Steelers that summer. My foot felt pretty good. I figured I only had to get my wind back to get into shape again.

I hadn't had any real exercise since being wounded, four months earlier. I thought I'd start with a light workout, so I set my alarm clock for an hour and a half before reveille.

It was a clear spring morning. I remember how the dew on the prairie grass glistened in the pale dawn light. As my footsteps crunched onto the cinder track, a needle of pain jabbed my right foot. The toes didn't bend much anymore. They didn't *look* bad. They just didn't work. I loosened up with some stretching exercises, then started jogging at an easy pace.

Within half a mile I was gasping for breath, struggling and stumbling.

"No!" I murmured in shock, remembering how easy a two-mile run had once seemed. "This can't be! *It can't be!*"

But I wouldn't give up.

Tough, agonizing weeks followed before I could run any distance. I didn't even worry about my lack of speed.

The Steelers, unfortunately, had to. I reported to preseason camp and took a beating. I was tired, sore, limping. When the coaches timed us in the 40-yard dash, their stopwatches put me dead last, slower than the biggest lineman in camp. And I was supposed to be a running back!

Head Coach Chuck Noll told me his decision. "It doesn't look like you've got a future with us, Rock," he said tersely. "Maybe you can build yourself up enough to try again next year."

Next year! How often does a comeback like that happen? How can a guy manage to become a better athlete while he's getting older, and sitting idle? I was five-feet-nine, too small for the pros anyway, everyone said. Maybe I should give up.

But I wouldn't. I underwent another operation, to repair damaged muscles and restore movement to my injured foot. And, though I took a job with a Chicago insurance firm, I still forced myself into a rigorous after-hours exercise program.

The worst days of football training camp are the first weeks—a period of tough physical workouts, twice a day. Even conditioned athletes sometimes collapse in the summer heat.

Well, I decided I would punish *myself* that way for the whole year. I exercised before work, at lunch breaks and in the evenings. At the end of a day, I had to force my legs up the steps of a railroad overpass on my running route. *Can't do this anymore!* my body cried; my will forced it on.

I punished my body every day for a year. I wanted to be a running back.

When the 1974 summer training camp opened, I reported early with the rookies to take advantage of the extra workout time. And there were some hopeful signs. Muscles that had been tight or useless the year before now surged with new strength; joints stiff before my operation felt loose and flexible again. My speed—never outstanding—was suddenly respectable. There was hope . . . I knew it . . . believed it . . . willed it.

Then the first day of regular camp, I pulled a hamstring muscle. There was this sharp, knifing pain in the back of my leg. Every athlete knows what that means—out of action, maybe for the season.

"You'd better think about hanging it up, fella," a team doctor advised me. "You'll only keep getting this sort of injury. That kind of scar tissue builds up in your leg. You want to ruin yourself for life?"

Even Coach Noll gently advised me: "Maybe you should think seriously about staying with the insurance business."

The message was there, plain as day: *Quit!*

I felt betrayed—by my own body. How could *it* do this to *me*?

Even though I knew the end of my athletic career might come any day, I accompanied the team up to Green Bay, where we were to play the Packers in an exhibition game. It was a chance to visit my family in Appleton, Wisconsin. And I could have a serious talk with an old friend, Father Al Lison. His six-foot-two frame was still lean, though his salt-and-pepper hair showed a bit more white, perhaps. But he was still the man who had guided me through high school. Father Al had the knack of asking the right questions and listening in the right places. In a few moments, after he'd seated himself in our kitchen, I was telling him everything that was on my mind. I told him about my year of sweat and uncertainty. I told him about my latest injury, and Coach Noll's suggestion.

"I guess it's time to decide whether you've tried long enough, Rocky," he said gently. "How do you feel about it?"

I didn't answer for a long time. Finally I said, "I made a promise back in Vietnam. When I was lying there wounded, I prayed that if I survived I'd do the best I could with my life. I didn't say I'd become a priest, Father." We laughed.

"I wouldn't make a good priest. But I thought I would make a good football player. I promised I'd keep on trying."

Father Al smiled. "I guess you're learning something about life now, Rocky. A lot of things require two wills—yours *and* God's. We used to talk about how the Lord must have had His hand on your shoulder, because of how well you did in high school and at Notre Dame, remember? Well, the hand's still there, Rocky. But do you feel it? Or are you just trying to make it on your own?"

It was a surprising idea. Maybe pure, hard grit and punishing training weren't enough.

I went back to the Steelers' camp with renewed determination—and something more. I was waiting to feel His hand on my shoulder.

No one was looking for me to be a star ball carrier, but there are many other jobs for a professional football player. When coaches asked me to block, I'd put my head down and do the job. When I was told to cover kickoffs, I tried to be the first man downfield. And each day that went by without reinjuring my hamstring, I breathed a silent "Thanks" to the Lord.

When the team roster was posted after final cuts, my name was on it. I'd made the Steelers!

Success didn't come in one big wave. Talking with Father Al had prepared me for the gradual, uneven way God's will can unfold in a person's life. So I lived with the restraints and setbacks. For several seasons, all the game action I saw was special team play—such as the kickoff team and punt coverage. When I was sent into the regular lineup, I was generally used as a blocker for another player. I didn't mind. I hadn't set any conditions on the direction of God's guiding hand. But the season, climaxed by the 1975 Super Bowl, still remains special to me. That was the first year I managed to break into the starting lineup. Besides blocking for our great 1000-yard rusher, Franco Harris, I became a useful part of our offense in my own right, running and catching passes.

I'll never forget the day of the Steelers' first Super Bowl game. It wasn't our victory over the Vikings in New Orleans I remember as much as a single moment before the game.

It was early. Most of the spectators had not yet crowded into the huge, open bowl of Tulane Stadium. I had put on my uniform and all alone silently walked through a passage out toward the field. At the mouth of the tunnel, I stopped and my heart jumped a beat.

"Lord," I said, "I can hardly believe You've put me here. The Super Bowl! I couldn't do it on my own. A lot of the players are out here today because they're fast or strong or naturally great athletes. I'm not any of those things. And now I realize—that's the gift You gave me. In Your will, my will worked."

Early in the fourth quarter, when the game was still close, Terry Bradshaw handed off to me. I was tired, late getting to the hole opened by our line—two Vikings closed it up. The lines slammed together. Dust, heat, sweat, tired bodies crashing together, punishing one another in an effort to triumph over the opponent. That's sport. I summoned up enough energy to step sideways, and found a bit of running room on my own—enough to make a first down.

As I walked back to the huddle, one of our linemen slapped his big hand on the top of my helmet and said, "Attaboy, Rock. Never give up. If we can't do it for you, do it on your own." Behind my face mask, I just grinned. I knew I could never do it on my own.

 # A Soft Voice in the Night
Brett Butler

Ever since I can remember I've always been the smallest guy around. In fact, many people told me I wasn't big enough to make it in the majors.

When I was growing up—first in Freemont, California, and later in Libertyville, Illinois—the bigger kids would chase me around the school yard. I remember their shouts: "Shrimp! Small-fry! Midget!" I'd run and run, and finally just run home.

Panting at our door, I'd scoop up the evening paper to check out the baseball news—box scores, stats, the daily pitching form. I could never get enough of baseball.

By the time I entered Libertyville High, I was only five feet, shorter than my *younger* brother. Still I went out for baseball. Surrounded by bigger kids, I hustled to make up for my lack of size. I beat out dribbling ground balls for infield singles, made diving catches and stole bases. But most of the time I perched dejectedly on the bench.

On Friday nights Dad, a lanky ex-Marine, would come in off the road from his salesman's job. Tired as he usually was, he'd put aside his newspaper to hear my tale of woe.

"Son," he said one night when I was feeling particularly low, "if you don't believe in yourself, nobody else will. Don't worry about your build. A wise man put it right when he said, 'Size is a matter of opinion.' "

He leaned forward in his chair and grasped my shoulder.

"You believe in your heart that you can play ball, don't you?"

"Yeah."

"Then go for it."

Something else happened to influence me. In the summer of 1973, when I was a high school sophomore, I attended a Fellowship of Christian Athletes conference in Fort Collins, Colorado. It was a good time, and an important time.

There one night I got down on my knees and prayed. That's when I began counting on Jesus. He gave me added confidence.

His help came alive through our high school FCA huddle groups in which we'd gather regularly to study the Bible, share worries, and find out how others faced their problems. I realized I wasn't the only one with troubles, with doubts and insecurities. That made my frustration over my height easier to deal with.

Yet I still rode the bench. I kept working hard, hitting, fielding and moving faster, always trying to be where I wasn't expected, playing aggressively. Still, I seemed to be the only one who believed in me.

One day at a game, I was squirming on the sidelines in the hot sun. The coach's favorite player was the catcher, whose brother was also on our team. The brother always played and it griped me to see him in my position in the outfield. On this particular day we were behind by three runs and I groaned every time he misjudged a ball or flubbed a throw. Finally, I ran up to the coach. "Look, you've got to give me a chance," I pleaded. "I'll *prove* I'm better!"

My outburst backfired. The catcher heard me and threw down his glove. The coach glared at me. For much of our final two seasons I remained on the second string.

With graduation near, I set my sights on Arizona State University, a big collegiate powerhouse from which many players were drafted for the majors. One day I asked our assistant coach about scholarship chances at ASU. He gazed out the window and said coolly, "Well, Brett, I wish you the best."

I mentioned it to our head coach too. I guess it was the wrong thing to do. On the night of the end-of-season banquet when the awards were handed out, as he was standing in front of everybody, the coach joked, "Well, here's Brett Butler getting his varsity letter and he thinks he's going to Arizona State when he couldn't even play for us."

The room whirled. Again I could hear the taunts—"Shrimp! Midget!"—and running feet pursuing me. Then, looking out into the sea of heads, one face became clear. It was Dad's. What a relief! He was smiling, shaking his head. He gave me a big wink, and I suddenly remembered how he had once said, "Don't ever let anybody tell you can't do something." I winked back at him.

I was more determined than ever. "As long as you play ball one hundred percent and do the best you can," Dad said, "we'll back you."

I went on to Arizona State but could only afford two years' tuition. I led the junior varsity in hitting, but a scholarship for the final two years was iffy. The baseball program was incredibly competitive.

I learned I could get a full scholarship at Southeastern Oklahoma State University. In fact, they were eager to have me come. But whoever heard of Southeastern Oklahoma? To me it was a small-fry school out in the boondocks. No major league scout would bother with a school like that. What was the point?

But Dad thought it might be a good opportunity, not as much competition as ASU. Durant, Oklahoma, however, was the last place this city boy wanted to go. No, I felt I should take my chances with Arizona State. Every day that summer I prayed about my tough decision. So did Mom and Dad. Big school versus little school—I didn't know what to do.

One hot night I lay in bed tossing and turning. It seemed like my whole future was at stake. A sweet summer breeze blew through the room. Then in a moment of quiet, it was as if someone spoke to me in the darkness, telling me I must go to Southeastern. *There's a reason*, the voice seemed to say. I sat up in shock. This was too strange. But I was sure I'd heard it. Climbing out of bed, I walked dazedly into the hall. I saw a familiar figure coming towards me. My mother. Something had roused her too. As she drew close I saw a look of amazement in her wide-awake eyes.

"You're going to Oklahoma, aren't you?" she asked.

"Yes," I replied softly.

Today I believe that reason was Don Parham, Southeastern's splendid athletic director. "Doc" Parham was a coach who put his players before anything else. He knew how to get the best out of each of us. He motivated me, and he paid no attention to my lack of physical stature. My confidence *soared*. In my first year the team made it to the championships of the National Association of Inter-collegiate Athletics. I learned enough from Coach Parham to become a two-time all-American. Eventually Coach Parham put in a word for me with a scout he knew. In 1979, my senior year, I was drafted by the Atlanta Braves.

It was another long climb up through the minor leagues before I finally made it to The Show, as we players call it. Along the way I faced many of the same questions and doubts regarding my size. But by now I knew to ignore the naysayers and depend on what had brought me this far—a wink and a good word from my dad, the patient self-confidence I'd found through a dedicated coach, and that occasional soft voice in the night that never steered me wrong.

 # Thanks for the Miracle!
Tony Conigliaro

Things were going great. It was the middle of August, 1967, and my team, the Boston Red Sox, was on its way to the American League pennant, the club's first since 1946. To make it even sweeter, we had finished ninth the year before, so our comeback was to become the greatest in the history of baseball.

Personally, I was in my fourth season in the major leagues and having one of my best years. I had hit 20 home runs and was batting around .280 with six weeks to go. I felt I had an outside chance of reaching my 1965 homer output—32, tops in the league that year. Here I was, only 22 years old, playing right field for the team I had idolized as a kid and having a ball—on and off the field.

Then suddenly, on the night of August 18, the roof fell in on me.

We were playing the California Angels in Boston, and Jack Hamilton, a hard-throwing right-hander, was pitching. When I came up to bat in the third inning, I checked the boxes behind our first-base dugout to make sure my family had made it to the game. Mom, Dad and my brothers, Billy and Ritchie, had come into town from Swampscott, Massachusetts, and when they saw me looking their way, they gave me a big wave. I smiled back.

Stepping into the batter's box, I took couple of practice swings and then set myself, waiting for Hamilton's first pitch. He let go with a fast ball, high and tight, too tight. The ball slammed against my left temple, and I went down in a heap. Though I was wearing a plastic batting helmet for protection, it was not equipped with a side flap, so my skull absorbed the full shock.

Grabbing my head, I squeezed it hard, trying to stop the shriek that filled it, and at the same time I was gasping for breath. There wasn't any air; it was as if I were strangling. "Oh, God," I prayed, "let me breathe. Let me live." A few minutes later they carried me into the locker room where Dad and Billy and Ritchie had come from the stands.

I heard Dad's voice, but couldn't find him. Everything was dark. Then I realized that I was blind.

"I can't see, Dad," I said anxiously.

"Take it easy, son," he answered, taking my hand. "You'll be all right."

"Sure you will," echoed Buddy LeRoux, the trainer, but in muffled tones I heard them whispering and I knew that my face must be a swollen mess. At the hospital, X-rays showed that I had a broken cheekbone, but I was more concerned with my sight.

Doctors, however, assured me that the blindness I was experiencing was normal. "It and the internal bleeding will clear up in a few days."

"Thank God," said Mom in a response that was full of a gratefulness we all felt.

Mother has been the spiritual counselor for our family for as long as I can remember, reminding us of our obligation to God. Grace at meals, bedtime prayers, church every Sunday all came like clockwork at our house because of her. So prayer was no stranger to me that night, and I asked God to make me well, but I tried to suggest that He hurry. I had to get back to the ball team.

My prayers were reinforced many times, I was to learn later. From all over the country came letters from fans who said they were praying for me.

Though sight returned to my right eye in about 48 hours, it was seven days before my left eye opened. When it did, the doctors discovered a blister had formed on it and then broken. A perforated retina resulted, and there was a strong possibility it would be permanently damaged. With this news, I began to really worry.

"What about baseball?" I asked. "I can't hit a ball seeing like this' Everything was blurred, and the sight in my left eye measured 20-300.

"We'll just have to wait and see," the doctors advised, avoiding telling me what they really felt.

Now, I'd played sports all my life and I had been in some tight spots before. "When the going gets tough, the tough get going," I told myself. If I went into a batting slump, I would go out to the park early for several days and take extra practice. Hard work, willpower, concentration, determination—they all had worked before.

Slowly, however, I discovered I was up against a new kind of problem. The World Series rolled around, and I was still stumbling over blades of grass. What a tough pill to swallow that was, watching my team in the World Series and not being able to play. Some players wait a lifetime for the experience. Still, I thought I'd be back in the lineup by spring training.

After the Series I went with some athletes to Vietnam to visit our servicemen in hospitals there. I suspect Joe DiMaggio and Jerry Coleman, the ex-Yankee greats, invited me to go along for my own therapy as much as for the troops', but regardless, I went and was glad I did. There I saw something that really jolted me—thousands of young guys about my age maimed for life, but they seemed to accept their situations with a courage and faith that put mine to shame.

I shall never forget one encounter—walking up to one young soldier who was in traction with his head just a ball of white bandages. Doctors had told me that his face had been shot away and that he would never see again. I tried to carry on a conversation with him, but a watermelon lump kept coming into my throat that made it impossible. Finally I took his hand and mumbled, "Stay in there pitching, Bob."

As I turned to go, he called after me, "Tony, how's *your* eyesight?"

Imagine—this guy blinded for life being concerned about a blur in one of my eyes. Something happened at that instant that shook me in a way I won't ever forget. God was trying to tell me something through that wounded soldier—that whether I ever played ball again or not, life went on and I had to find my place in it.

Yet baseball was my occupation, and I continued to pray for a healing so I could play again.

I struggled through the long winter, trying not to be bitter at the thought I would never play again. I wasn't mad at Jack Hamilton who had hit me. It wasn't his fault. Getting hit is sometimes a part of baseball. Nor did I feel that God had brought this on me. All I knew was that I was angry with frustration.

When spring-training time arrived, I went South and tried to play ball again, but there was nothing I could do right. At the plate, I swung and missed balls by a foot. The other players and coaches tried to be encouraging, but they couldn't fool me. I was pathetic and knew it. So I went back to Boston, where I had another examination.

"If anything, your sight is getting worse," the doctors said. I walked out of the building in a daze.

Face it, Tony, you're through, a voice inside me said. *Don't give up, have faith,* argued another. It was about this time that I had a chat with Father Johnson, my athletic director at St. Mary's High School in Lynn, Massachusetts, where I had played football, baseball and basketball.

"Don't let your heart grow cold toward God, Tony. Don't blame anyone. Be patient. Have faith and continue to ask for His healing."

"But it would take a miracle," I protested.

"Then," he answered calmly, "we will pray expecting a miracle."

I tried, but it was not easy.

The summer dragged on. I went out to the ball park in the mornings and worked out with a pitching coach, thinking I might be able to make a comeback as a pitcher. I had done some pitching in high school and thought it might be easier than hitting. But when the doctors heard about it, they told me I might be endangering my eyesight, so I had to quit. After that I stayed away from the ball park. I couldn't bear to watch a game and not play myself.

Near the end of the season, however, my doctor advised me that my eye problem had stabilized and gave me permission to go to Florida and try pitching in an instructional league. My pitching was lousy, but amazingly I found I could hit the ball again. It was only against minor-league players, and there is a big difference, but it was enough encouragement that I went back to Boston and the

Retina Foundation. There Dr. Charles Regan examined my left eye and exclaimed:

"I can't believe it. We've got a small miracle on our hands. Your vision is normal." Then, with a smile he added, "You must have been saying your prayers."

"Every day for a year," I answered.

That still didn't mean that I could win back my job on the Red Sox. Many players, after being hit, become gun-shy and aren't able to stand up to the plate without flinching. It has nothing to do with fear—it's psychological. I'd have to wait until spring training to find out.

In Florida the next spring, I put on my spikes again and gave it a try. Everything felt all right, and I didn't have any trouble seeing the ball. But my timing was way off, and I had to begin a terribly slow relearning process.

Then came the day in Tampa when I hit my first home run since the accident. It was a big turning point. After that my confidence grew, and improvement came more rapidly.

On opening day I was in the starting lineup in Baltimore, and what a thrill it was to be back! Any other year it would have been sort of routine, starting another seven-month season, but this time I was full of excitement. It was my rookie year all over again.

In the tenth inning, with the score tied, I came to bat against Baltimore pitcher Pete Richert. He delivered one over the heart of the plate, letter high. It was just the pitch I'd been waiting for, and I could tell the way the ball left the bat it was on its way: a game-winning home run!

That was a tremendous thrill, but there was still a bigger one in store for me a week later when we had our home opener in Boston. Fenway Park was packed. Mom and Dad and Ritchie and Father Johnson were in the stands. And my brother Billy was playing alongside me in the outfield that afternoon.

When I came up to bat the first time (the first time in Fenway Park since I had been hurt), the crowd rose to its feet and let go with one of the most deafening roars I ever have heard. I tipped my helmet and stepped up to the plate, but the din grew louder. The fans stamped and shouted and applauded more.

"Step out, Tony," the umpire said, waving me out of the batter's box. "You might as well let them get it out of their systems."

It's a good thing he called time, because I had something wet in my eyes and I couldn't have hit a pumpkin right then, let alone a baseball.

"Thank you," I kept saying over and over. It seemed so inadequate, but it expressed everything I had in my heart. "Thank you. Thank you for your prayers. Thank You, God, for a miracle."

Tony Conigliaro died on February 24, 1990.

 # With All Your Heart
Bill Curry

As a football coach, I've been guided by a number of tremendous people, and although I've worked with some of the best athletes and coaches around, the one person I think of most often had nothing to do with sports.

Miriam Berry was the choir director at our church, College Park Presbyterian outside of Atlanta. As a kid, I loved to sing and I had a good soprano voice. Big for my age and bursting with nervous energy, I frequently made life difficult for my teachers. One teacher became so frustrated with me that she tied me to my chair and taped my mouth shut. Not Mrs. Berry. Patient and caring, she had a way with her choristers that made us want to stay in our chairs even after rehearsals were over.

When I was 12 years old, Mrs. Berry asked me to sing the solo at our Christmas concert. She practiced the music with me until I had mastered every note and phrase. On the night of the concert I stood proudly before the congregation, my robe stiff with starch, my hair slicked down.

Then stage fright struck. As I stared at all those adult faces, my knees trembled, my throat went dry and I forgot the words I was supposed to sing. And yet, just as I began to stumble, another soprano voice picked up the words "If with all your hearts ye truly seek me." Mrs. Berry was singing for me, guiding me, backing me up, giving me the confidence I needed to continue on my own.

When the concert was over people came up to Mrs. Berry and me, saying, "What a lovely duet." Neither of us let on that it was supposed to be a solo.

Not long ago I visited Mrs. Berry again. Many years had passed since we sang together, but when she saw me, she remembered immediately. "Mendelssohn," she said. She was right. The lyrics of Mendelssohn's song ("If with all your hearts ye truly seek me . . .") are adapted from the Bible, and to me they remain an apt description of Mrs. Berry.

She loved me when I was hardest to love. She believed in me with all her heart. And that's good advice for getting the best from anyone. Whether you're coaching a football team or teaching a dozen squirming singers, do it *with all your heart.*

 # Life After Baseball
Dave Dravecky

I broke my left arm as a result of a pitch I threw in Montreal on August 15, 1989. It seemed at the time as if the whole country saw the gruesome replay that kept showing on television. It was a big story. It was also the end of my baseball career.

Looking at the replay now, I can still feel the pain that seared through the whole left side of my body like a lighting bolt. I remember a collective gasp rising from the stands as I tumbled over in a writhing heap on the hard, blue-green Astro Turf, and the horrified looks of my teammates on the San Francisco Giants who raced to the mound—first baseman Will Clark, catcher Terry Kennedy, trainer Mark Letendre, manager Roger Craig. Even the Expos batter, Tim Raines, trotted out. He'd heard the sharp crack of my arm snapping, like a pistol shot, all the way at home plate, 60 feet 6 inches away. And I remember closing my eyes and asking, "What can You possibly have in store for me now, Lord?"

It was a good question. That last pitch was more than the end of a playing career: It was the end of a sports drama that had played out over the previous weeks in front of a rapt national audience. It had culminated five days earlier, on August 10, in San Francisco's Candlestick Park, amid a deluge of media coverage, when I pitched—and won—my first major league game nearly a year after surgery for removal of a cancerous tumor in my pitching arm.

I will never forget the day Dr. George Muschler at the Cleveland Clinic diagnosed the tumor. It was September 23, 1988. My wife, Janice, was with me in the examining room as Dr. Muschler explained the surgery that would remove half of the deltoid muscle in my left arm, the large muscle that runs from your shoulder to your humerus bone.

Janice wanted to be very clear about what the doctors were telling us. "In other words," she said, her voice wavering slightly, "short of a miracle, Dave will never pitch again."

"That's right," Dr. Muschler replied sadly but absolutely. "Short of a miracle, he'll *never* pitch again."

God gave us that miracle. In the face of all odds, and without most of my deltoid muscle, I came back. The doctors couldn't figure out how I was doing it. They thought that after surgery I'd be lucky to be able to pull my wallet out of my back pocket. Just lifting my arm over my head would signal a remarkable recovery. Far from worrying about saving my career, they were focused on saving the *arm*. Yet in less than a year I was striking out major league hitters. Everyone called it unexplainable, but the explanation was clear to me. Dr. Muschler had said so himself: It could only be God answering prayer.

Why then, I wondered as I was carried off the field in Montreal that day, with players from both sides looking on in tears, had God done so much and brought me so far just to take back the miracle He'd given?

I'd been pitching baseball competitively since high school back in Boardman, Ohio, a quiet suburb of Youngstown. I did my hard time in the minor leagues, where pitching instructors gave me little chance of making the bigs. I endured dysentery and loneliness throwing winter ball in South America. It was there, in Barranquilla, Colombia, during the darkest days of my career, that I began to develop a spiritual yearning for something more in my life than the baseball diamond. There had to be a greater plan.

A year later, struggling in lowly Double A ball in Amarillo, Texas, I met someone who helped me start to find an answer. He was my roommate, Byron Ballard, a likable young pitcher. The first thing I noticed about Byron was that he had hair the color of saffron, with freckles to match, and size 15 feet. The other thing was that he spent most of his spare time reading and talking about the Bible. For a long time I listened and asked questions. Pretty soon I was reading the Bible too—devouring it. All that hot summer, while other players around me were cursing the hard, scorched infields and brutal game temperatures, the meager meal money and run-down motels, a change I had never dreamed was transfiguring my life and putting the world in an entirely new and startling perspective.

So seven years later, when the bad news about my arm came from Dr. Muschler at the Cleveland Clinic, it had been the most natural thing in the world for Janice and me to pray for a healing. As painful as the thought was of giving up baseball in mid-career, a career I'd worked so hard to build and was just beginning to enjoy the fruits of, we understood it would be completely up to God if I made it back. When the doctors insisted it was impossible, Janice and I knew better and said so. We trusted in the Lord's plan, whatever it was.

When my arm broke after my big comeback game, I was disappointed—all that sweat and pain just to pitch a handful of innings. But angry, no. I knew that God must have something else in mind. What, I wasn't sure. But like any athlete, the prospect of retirement was tough. The career of a ballplayer is relatively short. For most of us it is over way too soon. You grow up being a ballplayer; walking away from it in the prime of your life is the hardest thing you'll do, no matter how successful you've been. In the movie *Field of Dreams* one of the phantom old-time ballplayers who vanishes mysteriously into the cornfield after each "imaginary" game cries out in a joking imitation of *The Wizard of Oz*'s Wicked Witch: "Help me! I'm melting!" Melting away—that's how the thought of leaving baseball sounds to those of us who have been fortunate enough to play the game.

On November 13, 1989, I announced my retirement, at the age of 33. I'd broken my arm a second time that fall when I was inadvertently knocked to the field in the wild celebration that followed the Giants clinching the National League pennant. It was clear that without the deltoid muscle to help support it, my humerus bone was acutely vulnerable to stress fractures.

Not long after, doctors informed us that the tumor had returned. I would undergo another operation along with a new treatment that involved surgical implantation of "spikes" containing a small amount of radioactive material. This time I would lose the remainder of my deltoid muscle. In fact losing the whole arm was now a real and frightening possibility.

In the face of such an uncertain future, other things began happening in my life. I'd never particularly cared for all the media attention I got during my comeback. But the one good thing it did give me was a chance to say a few words publicly about my faith and to set an example for other cancer patients, many of whom suffered far more serious forms of the disease than I. Now people were asking me to speak all over the country—at churches, hospitals, business meetings. I was a bit embarrassed at how much in demand

I was. I wrote a book. Movie producers contacted me about doing my story. I was busier than ever.

It dawned on Janice and me that none of this could have happened if a small mysterious lump on my arm had not turned into something else. Which is not to say God gave me cancer—He didn't. But it was only through the love of God that I was led to find good in tragedy. The real miracle in my life was not that I came back from an impossible situation and played ball again. The real miracle in my life—in everyone's life—is that the Son of God came down to earth to suffer and die for our sins and redeem our souls. And that His love is always ready for us.

Inevitably there are times when I miss baseball, when I can practically hear the hum of the crowd as the players take the field. I see a game on television and immediately I am drawn into thinking how I would pitch the batter: slider on the outside corner of the plate, a change-up out of the strike zone, then *boom*, a fastball in on the hands. Keep 'em guessing. Sometimes it's just a feeling in the air on a humid summer night, the kind of night when a pitcher's arm can get warm and loose and great things might happen.

Last spring Janice and I returned to Scottsdale, Arizona, where the Giants train. Actually I was just along for the ride. Janice was speaking to a group of the baseball wives.

For a moment, when I first stepped into camp and heard the crack of wood on hard leather and saw a ball arc lazily into the deep desert sky, it was as if nothing had changed. I felt almost as if I could lace on my cleats again and go nine. But then just as quickly, before that ball smacked into the outstretched glove of a rookie outfielder, my separation from the game became crystallized and final, and I was at peace. It is a chapter of my life that's closed now. I am grateful for every second of it, especially those last few miraculous innings no one ever dreamed I'd get.

I've had several surgeries since my retirement. After each one there seems to be a little less of my left arm to save. I still may lose it. One thing I know. God never takes back a miracle. He just uses miracles in our lives to point the way.

In the spring of 1990, Dave Dravecky's left arm was amputated. He is the author of two books, Comeback *and* When You Can't Come Back.

Success on the Field of Life
Jimmy Evert

I'm a teacher. For more than 40 years my greatest enjoyment has come from helping people of all ages and from all walks of life learn and master the game of tennis. Some of my students have become champions, including my own daughter Chris. But long before Chris came on the scene, tennis had been my game, my livelihood—and my teacher.

Tennis has excited me ever since I was a nine-year-old perched on a curb outside the fence of the exclusive Town and Tennis Club in Chicago. My frayed knickers and worn Keds stood in stark contrast to the snowy pleated skirts of the women and the white linen trousers of the men playing tennis inside.

As the game ended and players began strolling back to the clubhouse, I called, "Any old balls, mister?" One of the men smiled and lobbed a ball over the fence to me.

"Thanks!" I hollered. Then I raced to the city's public-park hard courts and sold the ball for a nickel.

That scene became a regular ritual. My dad's job as a florist brought in just enough to keep Mom and us four brothers going. So with the extra nickels I got from selling old balls, I bought a used racket and began to play on the city courts and at my grammar school, St. Henry's.

One day as I was staring through the high grille fence of the Town and Tennis Club, a tall, friendly-looking man called to me: "Like a job, son?"

In seconds I was inside. That's when I met George O'Connell, the club's tennis pro. Soon I was chasing balls and filing the automatic ballserver. While I raced around the courts I kept one eye on Mr. O'Connell as he worked with the players.

"Footwork is vital," I heard him say. "You must keep your feet going right up to the instant you start your stroke, and be in position to return the ball."

He soon noticed my interest, and one day he gave me some pointers. I devoured them. Before long part of my job was hitting balls back to his pupils. From then on, during the summer I was on the courts from early morning until dark.

Mr. O'Connell was a stern taskmaster. But a lot of what I learned wasn't so much in what he said as in what I saw him do. And I was impressed by the fact that his actions meshed with what I learned at St. Henry's, especially from one particular nun, Sister Anne.

One steaming afternoon a frustrated club member failed to return a serve, and flung down his racket, glared at Coach O'Connell and swore violently. As startled players stared, I looked at Mr. O'Connell, who never used bad language. I saw his jaw muscles tighten. *Oh, oh,* I thought. But then the coach relaxed and said quietly, "Let's take a break."

As I watched the two walk off the court, the man apologizing, I remembered a lesson Sister Anne had taught us: " 'A wrathful man stirreth up strife,' children, as Proverbs fifteen, eighteen tells us, 'but he that is slow to anger appeaseth strife.' "

Holding the racket correctly was very important to Mr. O'Connell when recommending the proper execution of the stroke. "Above all, Jimmy," he stressed, "don't let your mind wander or become distracted by things going on around you on the court. *Concentrate* on what you're doing."

That reminded me of another of Sister Anne's admonitions: "A double-minded man is unstable in all his ways."

Hard, continuous work was George O'Connell's main emphasis: "If you're really serious about a sport, or any field you want to excel in, you must constantly *work* at it, make it your goal. You can't play tennis three months of the year, and then go out for football or baseball."

In different words, that's just what Sister Anne taught: "As Jesus told us, no man, having put his hand to the plow, and looking back, is fit for the kingdom of God."

Though I didn't know it then, I was learning not only how to be successful on the tennis court but also on the field of life. But I really was beginning to appreciate how much Sister Anne and George O'Connell gave of themselves to others.

When winter's snow closed the courts, I'd jump on a streetcar and travel across the city every day to 34th and Wentworth to a big armory where Mr. O'Connell managed an indoor tennis center. Concentrating on my goal, working hard every day, I began to win local championships. Mr. O'Connell had other young kids like me under his wing, but he wouldn't take a cent for teaching us. He never smoked or drank and this was another discipline we picked up from him. Out of the goodness of his heart he'd chauffeur us in his Oldsmobile sedan to tournaments around the country. Eventually I ranked in the nation's top five players under age 15 and then became number three in the 18-and-under category.

George's admonishment about hard work and sticking to your goals paid off. I won a full tennis scholarship to Notre Dame University. College would have been impossible otherwise.

However, World War II put the kibosh on tennis; you could hardly find a decent ball. I dropped out of college and joined the Navy, helping to train recruits in athletics. After the war, I returned to college and earned a degree in economics.

On graduating, I joined my folks, who had moved to Fort Lauderdale, Florida. I would have loved to continue playing tennis full-time, but in those days making a living in pro tennis was out of the question. There were very few open tennis spots, and only the top players made any money, usually in exhibition games.

When I heard of a job opening for a teaching pro at Southside Park, the city's public tennis courts, I jumped at the chance. I remembered what mentors like George O'Connell and Sister Anne had done for me. Besides, I liked the idea that Southside Park was not an exclusive private club. Anyone could go there. The job felt so right that it seemed as if God had held the door open just for me.

The city wanted someone who wouldn't move away during the summers and I promised to stay. That was in 1948, and except for a brief stint up north when I met my wife, Colette, I have been a teaching pro with the city of Fort Lauderdale ever since. As soon as I got the job, I began to work with folks the way George O'Connell worked with me. And in my case the experience turned out far better than being a tennis champ.

The city tennis center became the place where my five youngsters grew up. Colette and I spent a lot of time together with the children on the courts. It was where Christine Marie started playing when she was five years old.

It wasn't long before I could see Chris's potential as I watched her walk the baseline and outwait her opponent instead of taking a high-risk shot or rushing the net for a quick win.

But when little Chrissie started flying around the court, with blond pigtails bouncing, I kept having to correct her. I had coached her to hold her racket with one hand, yet when she went to the backhand side, she would invariably grab the racket with both hands.

"No, Chrissie, no," I would admonish her as she looked up at me through big brown eyes. "Always with one hand . . . *one hand.*" She always nodded, but when she thought I wasn't looking, out of the corner of my eye I'd see her go right back to using both hands.

Finally it dawned on me, just as if George O'Connell were standing beside me saying, "Jimmy, use your head." There was no way a tyke like that could effectively wield a racket with one little hand. I she needed two hands to control the racket, then by golly I'd help her develop a good two-handed backhand.

I could almost hear Sister Anne quoting Proverbs: "Give instruction to a wise man, and he will be yet wiser . . ." After all, teaching is more than just passing on knowledge and laying down rules. It's sizing up your students, evaluating their talents and then helping them develop those talents to the best of their abilities. I knew my daughter had talent.

Chris eventually became one of the first professional tennis player to use the two-handed backhand, which many other top players use to advantage today. With it she went on to win 1,309 career matches. Eighteen of these are Grand Slam titles, including three Wimbledon championships.

Meanwhile, I'm still here in Fort Lauderdale. Over the years I've turned down offers from some prestigious private clubs because I like it where I am. After all, I promised the city I'd stay, and as Sister Anne said, a man should always keep his promise. Or did George O'Connell say that?

Why I Keep Laughing
Joe Garagiola

One day shortly after I retired from baseball I was asked to help out at a luncheon honoring Stan Musial. My duty would be to introduce a lot of big names in St. Louis—athletes, businessmen, politicians. I was kind of scared. Most of my public speaking had been limited to hollering at umpires.

So I prayed about it. "Look, God," I said, "I'm going to need your help to keep the fear in my belly and off my tongue."

And sure enough He helped me—helped me use a bit of humor when bringing on the famous guests. The light approach seemed to loosen everyone up, including me.

Prayer and laughter. I learned both by example from my parents. My father and mother came to America from Italy and neither one ever really learned to speak English. Papa was a bricklayer who worked long, backbreaking hours to provide for his wife and two sons. In the best of times this wouldn't have been easy, but those were the Depression years when building jobs were hard to come by.

But though I grew up right in the middle of this period, I never knew what the word *depression* meant. In our home there was faith in God and a smile for every situation—faith to banish fear and a joke to take the growl out of an empty stomach. That doesn't mean my brother and I didn't have to do without a lot of things. I remember how long it took me to convince Papa that I needed a pair of spiked baseball shoes. Papa couldn't understand why anyone would buy a new pair of shoes that he couldn't wear to church.

On the Hill, a section of St. Louis that is predominantly Italian, life centered around the church, as it does in most Italian neighborhoods. Saturday was take-a-bath, get-to-church-for-confession, help-mamma-fill-out-the-collection-envelope day. Mass the next morning was the high point of every week. It was a joyful occasion, not a solemn one. Church was where you met your friends, where the guys hung out.

This kind of natural-as-breathing religion was all the more important when I entered major league baseball. When a ballplayer hits .300 for the season, which means he gets three hits every ten times he comes to bat, everybody says he's had a great year. But this also means he's failed seven times out of ten. In a job where success means failing most of the time, you better have a faith that sees things in perspective.

And you'd better learn to laugh at yourself. I always liked Erne Fazio's answer when someone asked him why he'd switched from a 34-ounce bat to a 29-ounce bat. "Because it's lighter to carry back to the bench when I strike out."

I remember one close ball game when the other team had a runner on every base. Tension was building and I went out to the mound. There was a big hush over the field and then all at once I heard someone shout from the other team's dugout, "Hey, Joe, the only thing you know about pitching is that it's hard to hit." Suddenly my own importance and the spot we were in were cut down to size.

In baseball failure isn't only built into the game. There are personal setbacks and disappointments too. One year I got off to a good start only to break my shoulder in May and miss almost all of the rest of the season. The next year I was traded. After growing up in St. Louis and playing for the Cardinals in a World Series, it had just never occurred to me that I might have to leave them. Worse yet, it meant moving from a winning ball club to the Pittsburgh Pirates which had clinched last place that year on the opening day of spring training.

It's easy to laugh about that trade now, but believe me, at the time it would have been far easier to cry. I think the person who helped me most to keep my sense of humor then, and during the trades that followed, was my wife Audrie. "Dad's modeling uniforms," she'd explain to the kids each time I changed clubs.

Like laughter, prayer works better too when you have someone to do it with. I never went in much for "professional" praying—asking God to help my team win or to let me get a base hit. I'd always think, *What if the pitcher out there is praying for a strike-out while I'm asking for a home run?* My boyhood pal Yogi Berra put it well once in a game between the Yankees and the Red Sox. Jimmy Piersall came to the plate and made the sign of the cross before stepping into the batter's box. Yogi watched from his catcher's crouch, then said, "Why don't you let God just *watch* the ball game?"

Audrie's and my prayers are more often for strength in daily life, for joy and love in our family, for others in need, for God's gift of a merry heart. If you can smile and pray, you're part way there. If you have someone to pray with, and share that smile with, you've reached home plate.

 # A Quiet Reminder

Steve Garvey

In Tampa, Florida, where I grew up, my grandmother, Philippine Winkler, lived with us. Dad worked as a city bus driver, and to help make ends meet, Mom worked as an auto-insurance adjuster. Both of them were gone during the day, and so I was home alone with Grandma a lot when I was young. That worked out well for both of us.

Grandma depended upon me to be her hands. As a young woman, she had been walking on a sidewalk when a tire spun off a speeding truck and struck her, causing severe injuries that left her with a neurological affliction. Grandma's mind was keen, but she walked slowly and could not use her hands. She couldn't write a letter, dial a phone or turn on a gas stove.

With Dad and Mom gone all day, I would answer the phone, comb her hair, even cook dinner at times. Grandma would recite the recipes, and I would carry them out, measuring and mixing the ingredients and putting them in the oven.

Before I went out to play ball, I'd make lunch for her, put a straw in her drink and let her know where I'd be. If she needed me, she could call. A bell with a string attached hung outside the house. If I was close she'd just tug on it with her mouth. If I was too far away to hear, she'd flick on the porch light with her chin. More than once I'd be at bat when one of the kids would shout, "Steve, *the porch light is on.*"

For a moment I'd be tempted to disregard the call. But I couldn't. Not only would I be letting Grandma down, but I knew I would be letting something inside me down too. So, dropping the bat, I'd dash home. Always it would be something important, such as when the plumbing sprang a leak or a delivery receipt needed to be signed.

The porch light is on. Those words have a way of popping up in my mind at odd moments. For all these years, they've been a quiet reminder that we should all think of others, and that I myself should try to be the man God wants me to be.

 # Decisions, Decisions
Joe Gibbs

As a football coach I must make decisions, lots of them, quickly and almost constantly. I don't always make the right ones—no one does—but my record is pretty good, and that's partly because of a lesson I learned years ago.

At the time, I was offensive coordinator of the Tampa Bay Buccaneers. I was 38 and had been on the coaching staffs of college and professional football teams for 14 years. It was about time, I believed, I made head coach somewhere. But nothing seemed forthcoming.

Then Coach Don Coryell of the San Diego Chargers invited me to join him as assistant coach. As I usually do when making decisions, I prayed for guidance, discussed it with my wife, Pat, and sought confirmation in Scripture. Everything seemed right about taking the job.

But after I had accepted it, second thoughts crept in. Was it really right for me? After all, the new job wasn't a step-up, not even a lateral move, since an assistant coach didn't have the responsibilities of coordinator. And being coordinator usually puts one in line for head coach.

The more I brooded about it the more doubtful I became. Finally I decided to fly up to Fayetteville, Arkansas, to talk to an old Sunday school teacher who had been a mentor to me when I coached the University of Arkansas Razorbacks, and I felt he could give me some guidance.

On a January morning I caught a plane for Fayetteville, but we couldn't land there because of a snowstorm. We were diverted to Fort Smith, about 50 miles south. And that's where the circus started.

In a mixture of frustration and confusion, I rushed out of the airport looking for a taxi or bus, but nothing was available because of the snow. Then I spotted two men climbing into a car; one of them mentioned Fayetteville. Impulsively I rushed up and asked to accompany them. The men nodded, and off we went.

We hadn't traveled more than 15 minutes when I could see we would never make Fayetteville. We were slewing all over the highway, and it was clear that the driver had never driven in snow before. "Please stop," I asked. "I'm getting out."

The driver obligingly pulled over. I climbed out into the snow, crossed to the other side of the highway and flagged down an oncoming pickup. Back in the Fort Smith airport, I realized how stupid I had been. With a half hour before my return flight home, I slumped into a waiting-room chair, feeling completely defeated.

"OK, Father," I prayed. "I've really made a mess of things."

Something caught my eye on the chair next to me. I was surprised to see a Gideon Bible. With a sense of relief, I picked it up and turned to the first chapter of James, which has always been of special help to me. I was reading James's teaching that he who doubts God's guidance "is like a wave of the sea, blown and tossed by the wind" when a voice sounded in my ear: "I claimed that chapter about six months ago."

I turned and looked up in surprise at a stranger sitting next to me. "I'm a pharmacist who recently left my job for a new one in another state," he said. "I had prayed about it and the Lord had given me a green light. But I discovered I had to take a pharmacy examination by my new state's board to become accredited."

He shook his head. "It had been over ten years since I graduated and my chances of passing were practically nil. That's when I really began to doubt my decision." I smiled knowingly.

"Well," he continued, "I cranked up my faith and took the exam."

"What happened?"

"It was like a miracle," he answered quietly. "I passed with one of the highest scores ever registered. And, you know, I'm convinced it happened in order to remind me that when you ask God about a decision, you must trust Him and not worry about the outcome."

I stared at him, dumbstruck. I had made this foolish journey because I had second-guessed God, letting my own ambition take over. I hadn't needed to visit my old Sunday school teacher. This stranger had given me the answer I was seeking.

My plane-boarding announcement boomed over the loudspeaker. Standing up, I warmly shook the pharmacist's hand and soon was on my way home. As my plane sped through the night I knew exactly what I would do. I would go to San Diego with an open, enthusiastic heart and do my very best with the new job given me. I would trust God, just as I had meant to do in the first place.

Two weeks after I started in San Diego, the team's offensive coordinator left, and I was given his post. Two years later I was tapped as head coach of the Washington Redskins.

I have never again seen or heard from my pharmacist friend, but I believe the Lord has one of His angels filling prescriptions somewhere. I know he filled the right one for me.

Conditioning Ourselves Spiritually
Frank Gifford

(Written in 1957, while playing for the New York Giants)

To handle the tension that comes before every football game, I've worked out a formula. Although quite simple, it is every bit as important to me as making sure my shoulder pads fit securely.

I find myself a quiet corner in either the locker room or the training quarters, and take just a few minutes for a silent prayer. The prayer itself, rather than being a request to perform well, is one of thankfulness that I have been given the physical ability to take part in something I sincerely love to do.

When I was in high school and later in college, I used to be somewhat embarrassed, and would always look for a place in which to offer my prayer as far away from my teammates as possible. Then I discovered that other players were also wandering off to some quiet spot for the same purpose.

One of the highlights of my football career was being invited to play in the 1954 All-Pro Game (similar to baseball's annual All-Star game) in the Los Angeles Coliseum; I'll never forget an incident that happened before the game.

Players and coaches had finished pre-game discussions, when Abe Gibron and Lou Groza, two stars of the Cleveland Browns, stood up and asked the entire team if they would mind waiting just a moment.

"It's a custom with us to have a moment of prayer together before each game," said Groza.

With that, each of those 250-pound goliaths dropped on one knee and bowed his head.

When one of the referees entered the locker room to tell us we were holding up the game, our whole ball club was kneeling for two minutes of prayer. I have often wondered what he thought then, and later, as we meshed together perfectly to beat the Western All-Stars by a wide margin that day.

You spectators, if you have field glasses, watch the pre-game huddles of professional, college, or high-school games and notice the many players whose eyes were closed and lips moving. I notice it before every game the New York Giants play.

More and more athletes realize today that not only is body conditioning necessary, but also the spiritual conditioning of their minds. In football, as in life, you get knocked down and suffer losses from which you must recover. This takes good physical equipment and the proper mental outlook.

When I first joined the New York Giants back in 1952, I felt I could never be anything but a defensive back, that I could not run, pass or kick well enough to make the team. I told this to the Giant coach who took me at my word, figuring that if I had no confidence in my offensive skill, he certainly wouldn't. So for several years I played a defensive halfback only.

Then during one of my pre-game prayers, it occurred to me that it was primarily a lack of faith that limited me to one role in football. So I asked God, not to make me a good runner or passer, but simply to help me to use all of the abilities which He had given me in a maximum way.

This prayer changed my attitude. The new attitude was followed by action. I began using workouts to practice running, kicking, passing. Soon the chance came for me to play offensive halfback in a game, and I was able to make the grade.

If I have learned anything about prayer it is this: when the game is close and I have a chance to score the winning touchdown in the last minute of play, an emergency call to God won't get it for me. What will, is determined by how well I have prepared myself physically and mentally over a period of months.

In other words, I don't see how one can expect miracles from an emergency prayer if he hasn't bothered to develop a closeness to God when things were going all right.

Just as a football player could never amount to anything without physically conditioning himself, so too am I convinced that our prayers will not be effective unless we spiritually condition ourselves through life.

 # Trusting in the Lord
Steve Jones

When people learn I have a heart problem, they're surprised. I play a 32-week schedule of professional golf, and every day I have irregular heart palpitations that last four or five seconds. Twice I've had to cope with a condition called atrial fibrillation. It can act up at the most inopportune times.

In 1978 I was a college freshman and suddenly collapsed days before a big golf tournament. The doctors made their diagnosis, and I was put on bloodthinning medication and given cardioversion—electrical shocks to slow my heart back down to its regular rhythm.

The one question I had: Could I still play golf? Yes, I was told. Even so, the doctors didn't know if the condition would come again or had disappeared entirely. The palpitations could be frightening and debilitating. During atrial fibrillation, my energy was reduced drastically and my heart beat 90 to 140 beats per minute.

Several years ago I was finishing up at the Hardee's Classic in Moline, Illinois. My wife, Bonnie, and I were packing our suitcases to leave late the next day, when I felt the familiar, rapid, irregular heartbeats. I went right to bed.

The next day, before starting, I sought out the doctor at the tournament medical trailer. In the hot, sticky weather, I felt sweaty and dizzy. The doctor confirmed my fears, and Bonnie and I drove to the hospital, where I was given some medication and some mild electrical shocks.

After a week I was no better. The shocks didn't work and the medication didn't help. At the International, I was still walking around the golf course like a 95-year-old man. I always pray during a tournament, but this time I prayed more than ever.

Finally I checked into intensive care for some stronger shocks. When I was under anesthesia, it took the doctors three tries, increasing the intensity each time. That worked, and two weeks later I was back on the course.

If my condition couldn't be corrected, my days as a touring professional would be over. Of course, it's risky. There are risks involved in any job, from the emotional wear and tear in an executive's stress-filled life to the physical danger an assembly-line worker faces. But I enjoy playing golf. It's what I do. It's my profession. It's the talent I've been given in trust to develop, and so entrusted, *I trust in the Lord.*

 # A Restless Heart
Tom Landry

Defeat is never easy to take, but our loss to Cleveland in the National Football League play-off on December 22, 1968 was the biggest disappointment in my 30 years in football. I thought our team could go on to win the Super Bowl. Instead, we took a complete beating, 31 to 20, in the first elimination round.

During the plane ride back to Dallas after the game, I walked up and down the aisle, examining injuries and trying to console those players most upset by the defeat. But it wasn't easy; I felt pretty upset myself. When we arrived at the Dallas terminal, I wished each player a happy Christmas, then drove wearily home.

Before going to bed that night, I sat down in my bedroom chair to review the whole day. Not a pragmatic review, but a spiritual assessment. "Lord, what went wrong today?" I asked.

As almost always happens during these sessions with Him, I soon found perspective. A crushing setback today, yes, but I've learned that something constructive comes from every defeat.

I thought over my relationships that day with the players, coaches, officials, friends, family. Nothing wrong here. No bad injuries either. "Thank You, Lord, for being with me out there," I said.

And with that prayer the bitter sting of defeat drained away. Disappointment remained, but I've found that it doesn't sap energy and creativity. One football game, after all, is quite a small fragment of one's total life.

My father said the same thing to me back in 1939 when I was a high-school player in Mission, Texas. A Sunday-school superintendent in the Methodist church for 37 years, he tried to broaden my interests, but I wasn't listening then. Football was my whole life; the rational, scientific approach was my method.

In high school my dream was for our school to win the district football championship. We did, and I was chosen all-district halfback. But those achievements didn't seem to satisfy the restlessness which had entered my heart.

At the University of Texas I became co-captain of the football team, and in separate years we beat Alabama in the Sugar Bowl and Georgia in the Orange Bowl. All the things I could have dreamed for, yet they weren't enough.

Could I make it in the big time of professional football? I did—with the New York Giants. But the restless craving was still inside me.

When my football-playing days were over and I became a full-time coach on the New York Giants in 1956, I used my college training in industrial engineering to devise a complex—and, as it turned out, highly successful—system of defense that had never been tried before in professional football. Another accomplishment, but the sense of dissatisfaction remained.

After the 1958 football season, I returned to Dallas where my wife, Alicia, and I had settled. I was 33 years old; I had achieved almost every goal I had aimed for and had every reason to be happy and content. Yet inexplicably there was an emptiness in my life.

One day a good friend, Frank Phillips, casually invited me to attend a men's breakfast at the Melrose Hotel in Dallas. "I think you'll like it, Tom," he said. "We probe into the Scriptures and have some good fellowship together."

I had been in and about the church all my life, but only halfheartedly. And I wasn't sure Bible discussion was for me, since my scientific approach found it hard to accept certain parts of Scripture.

We met at 7:30 on a Wednesday morning in a private dining room at the hotel. There were four tables of eight to ten men. After breakfast the men at each table chose their own moderator who kicked off the discussion. What happened in the weeks that followed is not easy to explain. But I do know that these informal sessions of probing, questioning and searching the Gospels together began a whole new era in my life.

In looking back, I find it hard to pick out any one specific turning point. But my early attention was certainly grabbed by this passage:

Therefore I tell you, do not be anxious about your life, what you shall eat or what you shall drink, nor about your body, what you shall put on. Is not life more than food, and the body more than clothing? (Matthew 6:25 RSV).

Is not life, then, more than football? I asked myself uncomfortably. Challenged by this statement, I turned my thoughts to the Challenger. Who was He, this Jesus? Did I accept Him, really? For, I reasoned, *if* I accepted Him, then I accepted what He said. And if I accepted what He said, then there was something unsatisfying in the way I was living my life.

At that point I nearly stopped going to those Bible sessions. For my life had been carefully structured through the years, and I was quite convinced that my future lay in being a football coach. This was no time to become confused about my goals in life. But something kept me going to those breakfasts.

Another passage also caught me:

Every one then who hears these words of mine and does them will be like a wise man who built his house upon the rock; and the rain fell, and the floods came, and the winds blew and beat upon that house, but it did not fall, because it had been founded on the rock (Matthew 7:24 RSV).

Was my house founded on a rock? I thought about my wife, Alicia, and children—Tom, Jr., Kitty, Lisa. We were churchgoers; what did it really mean to us? What kind of a foundation was I building for my family? For a self-centered person, those can be disconcerting questions. Once again I turned my attention to the Challenger. For the first time I began to feel a quickening desire to get to know this Man. At the next breakfast, I asked, "How can we be sure Jesus is Who He says He is?"

No one could answer in a way that satisfied me, so I began doing research and reading about Jesus on my own. As a football coach, I measure things in terms of results. You train players to accomplish certain objectives—a place kicker to put three points on the scoreboard on most tries within the 50-yard line, a passer to throw the ball so that his receiver can catch it, and so forth. During each game we keep a chart on the players' efficiency in carrying out their assignments. If most players perform well, we will probably win the game.

Therefore, I couldn't help thinking about Jesus also in terms of what He did—of the results of His life. And the impact of His life on the lives of countless millions down through the years is impressive, compelling!

The results of my seeking brought me into confrontation with another fact. What Jesus Christ stood for was so much bigger than any goal or dream I ever had. Was I to go with Him or continue on my own? If I decided for Him, then it meant giving up my own desires, perhaps even football. It was nothing you decided casually.

The moment of decision? Here again I can't pinpoint it by time or place. There was no emotional experience. As the story of this Galilean evolved during these early-morning sessions, I found myself drawn to Him. Then at some period during the spring of 1959, all my intellectual questions no longer seemed important, and I had a curiously joyous feeling inside. Internally, the decision had been made. Now while the process had been slow and gradual, once made, the decision has been the most important of my life. It was a commitment of my life to Jesus Christ and a willingness to do what He wanted me to do as best I could by seeking His will through prayer and reading His word.

The result was that I learned what He meant when He said, *I came that they may have life, and have it abundantly (John 10:10 RSV).* He didn't ask me to give up football or my ambition to be the best coach in the business, but to bring Him into my daily life, including football. So I began to think a little less about football systems and a little more about the people involved.

Soon after I became coach of the Dallas Cowboys in 1960, I decided that I needed to take a stand for my faith before my own players. "A man needs to believe in Someone bigger than he is," I began. Then I told them of the decision I had made to put God first in my life.

There is now a team prayer session before every game. On Sunday mornings we encourage players to attend a service of their own faith. While playing away from home, we hold an early-morning nondenominational service before we begin our game preparation.

The desk in my office is round—just the right size for the other Dallas coaches and me to sit around and test strategy and ideas on one another. The subject matter is different, but the close fellowship reminds me of those Wednesday breakfast sessions almost 11 years ago. Jesus instructed us to operate this way and set the example by sharing His life with 12 disciples.

Once a decision is made for Him, it's amazing how differently you look at your family, your friends, your victories and defeats, at all of life. I begin each day now with a person-to-Person effort to contact Him. "Lord, I need your help today when we make our squad cuts," or, "Please give me the right words to say to the coaches at our meeting," or, "Help me to forget football today when I'm with Alicia and the children." At the end of the day, I take inventory. Was my criticism of the quarterback handled right? Did I get across to the squad my moral convictions without preaching? Was I too stern with Kitty over her last report card? The main evaluation concerns whether I had brought the Lord into these situations or whether I was barging ahead on my own.

When I get out of touch with Him, I flounder; power seems to ebb away, and that restless feeling returns. When God is in control of my life, that gnawing sense of dissatisfaction is gone, and I know for myself what Augustine, that great fifth-century saint, meant when he wrote, *Our hearts are restless until they find their rest in Thee.*

 # Caring Makes a Difference
Tommy Lasorda

Soon after I took over as manager of the Dodgers in 1977, sportswriters began to comment on how I'd pal around with my players and sometimes hug them unashamedly on the field in front of thousands of fans.

I started reading criticisms such as: "You can't get too close to your players and be a good manager. If you get too friendly with them, it'll be impossible to maintain any kind of discipline. They'll interpret it as a sign of weakness and take advantage of you. It's human nature."

That's the sort of talk that bugs me about sports today. Ever since Leo Durocher remarked some 30 years ago that "nice guys finish last," it seems to me that a lot of people connected with sports have been trying to prove it's true. Well, I just don't believe it. I love baseball, and I'm just naturally enthusiastic about the game, and when the chance came at last to manage a major league team—after 29 years of working and hoping—I was ready to put my theories on the line.

Now, every manager has his own way of running a ball club. Some lay down strict rules and keep tight control over their players on and off the field. I wanted to pattern the Dodgers after a family—a family that loves and respects one another, a family that wants to do things together and prays together.

I suppose this idea of "family" in baseball came from my own background. I've been blessed with my loving wife of 28 years, Jo, and two wonderful kids, Laura and Tom Jr. I don't fail to tell them how much I love them and appreciate them. I feel that's important, especially because they've had to put up with a lot from me—mostly not having me at home a good deal of the time because of all the road trips during almost three decades with the Dodger organization.

But it goes back even further, to when I was growing up in Pennsylvania, where my dad was a truck driver for a Bethlehem Steel quarry near Norristown. There were five sons in our family. Our parents were Italian immigrants and we loved them. I wasn't ashamed to kiss my father every time I greeted him, and all of his sons would have gone through fire for him.

But if we got out of line, he'd lower the boom on us. Discipline, yes—but loving and caring were the things that held our family together. Why, I asked myself, shouldn't the same principle work with the Dodgers?

Well, to my enormous satisfaction the Dodgers got right off to a big lead that year. Then one day a cynical reporter asked me right out, "What do you mean, you 'love' your players? What do you mean, you're 'close' to them?" I could tell he wasn't buying it—he felt somebody was putting him on.

I didn't answer him directly; instead I began a rundown: "Steve Yeager's wife is Gloria, and they have no children; Johnny Oates' wife is Gloria, too, and they have a daughter, Lori, and a son, Andy; Jerry Grote's wife is Sharon and his son is Jeff and his daughters are Sandy and Jennifer; Steve Garvey's wife is Cyndy and his daughters are Krisha and Whitney . . ."

I went through the whole roster. I think I bored the pants off him, but he got the idea—I really am close to my players. And they know the difference between feeling cared about and just being a number or a valuable property. Caring—that's the important thing.

Reggie Smith is a good example of what caring can do. Reggie had been with St. Louis and Boston, and by the time he came to the Dodgers, Reggie had a reputation as an uncooperative malcontent.

I was coaching third base at the time, and I kept hearing bad things about Reggie Smith this and Reggie Smith that. I realized he was tough—there isn't a guy in the world who can knock a tear out of him. Yet I remembered seeing him cry when he got word that his father was critically ill. I filed that away for future reference. It was obvious that he loved his father.

I began to notice other things. Reggie would bring his son, Reggie Jr., into the clubhouse to meet the other players; he was proud of that boy. And after the game he'd always greet his wife, Ernestine, and his daughter, Nicole, with a kiss, and he'd greet his brothers warmly. I said to myself, "This is a family man; he's a good man, a loving man." And I refused to believe any of the mean talk about him.

Then, when I became manager, I called him aside and said, "Reggie, I want to do a good job with the team. I *need* you."

Reggie put his arm around me and said, "Tom, I'll never let you down." And he kept his word. He was a super guy and a super star all season long. In fact, he broke Duke Snider's long-standing Dodger slugging record, and the fans voted him our team's most valuable player.

Reggie's super effort for the team seems to bear out a lesson I learned from the Bible, because I believe what a manager needs most of all, just as Solomon said, is "an understanding heart." (I Kings 3:9) That year I kept praying to God for an understanding heart in my dealings with people. I must have been doing something right because we went right through the season, winning our division by ten games.

I'm not naive enough to think this team won because of me. I never got a base hit for this team. I never scored a run or struck anybody out for this team. The players did that. And even though we didn't win the big one, we still had a very successful season.

Naturally we were disappointed that we couldn't bring the World Series championship to Los Angeles, but we didn't lose our sense of humor over the loss. In our gloomy locker room after Reggie Jackson blasted our hopes with his three homers in the final game, I told the Dodgers, "I still think you're the best ball team in the world, and I wouldn't trade you for any team *anywhere*." I paused, then added, "By the way, I hear there's a *great* team in Red China . . ." That broke the whole team up.

Afterward a writer cornered me and asked if I was going to change my tactics now. "Look," I told him, "in spite of what Vince Lombardi once said, winning isn't the only thing. Is it wrong that I tell my players that I love them? Is it wrong that I enjoy being around them? Isn't that what Jesus was talking about when He said, 'Love one another as I have loved you'?" And the writer just stared at me, as though he couldn't believe what he was hearing. But I meant every word of it. I still do. And I always will.

 # The Lift I Needed

Janet Lynn

I never expected what happened in Sapporo, Japan.

When I went there for the 1972 Winter Olympics a lot of people were counting on me to bring back a gold medal.

You can imagine the pressure this builds. Everyone you know talks about it; you read it in the newspapers. I didn't let myself think much about it, but deep inside I sort of hoped to win one, too.

Before any competitive meet, the pressure really intensifies. But it's the day you skate that you can really get in trouble. You can sit there going over and over your routine until you get so uptight your head swims.

My competition at the Olympics was to take three days. The first two for school figures, and the last for free skating. There are 64 different school figures—such as the eights, counters, rockers and paragraph threes. And you must know each one perfectly, because in competition you are assigned only six. Only at the last minute do you know which six they are.

The first day I did fairly well. And I vowed to do better the next day. But I had put myself under such tension that I didn't do as well at all. Sure I had prayed—prayed to win. And the Lord showed me after each figure that day how far off the track I was. In the middle of the second day of figures I was almost in hysterics, ready to quit.

We had a little room where we rested. Mom and my coach, Miss Slavka Kohout, came in to calm me. But it didn't help.

That evening at the Olympic Village, I lay on my bed crying and praying, wondering where I'd gone wrong. As I prayed I seemed to hear a soft voice: "Cast your burden upon Me, Janet. I still love you."

I drew a deep breath, remembering that moment when I first met Him. It was at a church camp in Lake Geneva, Wisconsin, where I had asked the Lord Jesus to come into my heart.

"Remember, Janet," said my counselor then, "Jesus is always with you, wanting to help you. When you suffer from fears or feelings of inferiority, just give them to Him. He promised to take them and give us peace.

"Don't forget," she emphasized, "He can handle *anything*. He doesn't want you crippled by inhibitions, worries or cares."

Now I knew what was wrong. As I had done so many times before, I'd forgotten His help and ended up hugging all my fears and inadequacies to me.

Right there in my room I relaxed and let my negative feelings float up to Him. It was like being loosened from a vise. It all became so clear. The Lord seemed to say: "Janet, it doesn't matter whether you get a gold medal or not; I just want you to skate for Me."

On the next day—my most important day—I felt good. My free-skating program was scheduled for the evening. So I had almost a whole day in which to get uptight. Instead, I just relaxed, didn't do much except talk with teammates, and sit quietly in my room and have fellowship with Him.

Whenever those fear-thoughts would start creeping in, I'd pray: "Lord, I know I needn't worry now about how I'll do tonight. I *know* You will give me the right feelings at the right time."

When I stepped out on the ice in front of those 8000 people, God did give me those feelings—a sense of freedom and love. Then, as I skated little circles to get the feel of the ice, I could hardly believe it. For suddenly I could feel His Spirit descending on me like a warm blanket of love. I felt free.

All I wanted to do was tell a story. That's what my coach always says as I step onto the ice: "Go out and tell a story!" And that's what I try to do in free skating.

Miss Kohout and I choreograph my program. We choose various selections of classical music, put them together on tape, and I interpret it in skating. The judges decide on composition, style and technical merit. It's a four-minute combination of ballet and skating gymnastics.

As I launched into my program, whirling and leaping, I felt wonderful. I didn't care about material things. I just wanted to skate my best for Him, for joy and love.

And then a strange thing happened. I fell.

In front of the whole world watching on television, I fell.

It happened in a flying sit spin, right in the middle of my program.

But an even stranger thing happened.

I hardly noticed it. In fact, I lifted right into my most difficult jump and finished the program well enough so that it helped me earn the Olympic bronze medal.

Afterward Miss Kohout and I watched my program on videotape to analyze what had happened; I had never fallen before in a sit spin in competition and hardly ever in practice. We figured it happened because I had launched my previous jump in the wrong place on the ice and thus started my preparation for the sit spin at a wrong angle.

More important, I thought of what would have happened if I'd reacted to the fall in my old way. Shame and embarrassment would have flung themselves at me with an accusatory, "You fell!" and I would have blown my program.

I went to the window of my room and looked up to the beautiful snow-covered mountains around Sapporo. And I thought of how He is always there to lift us.

For in completely giving ourselves to Him, He gives us back the best part of ourselves so we can face whatever life brings us.

 # Brothers

Kevin Maas

I sat in the dugout, waiting. It was Friday evening, June 29, 1990, and I was going into my first game in the majors—I'd just been called up to the Yankees.

How quickly things had moved. Just a day earlier I had been on the road in Richmond, Virginia, playing with the Columbus Clippers, the Yankees' Triple A team. Now here I was at Comiskey Park, in Chicago, playing the White Sox.

Pretty quickly I was on deck—I was the designated hitter, so I *had* to do well at bat—and then I was at the plate, feeling as though my legs didn't belong to me. Everybody in Comiskey Park was eyeing me. And all the time I was thinking, *If only Jason were here* . . .

Right from the start, back home in Castro Valley, California, Jason and I were a team, the Maas brothers. He was a year and a half older, but we were so alike in looks and ability that people mistook us for twins (they still do). For sure, we could compete tooth and nail playing ball in the front yard, but where it counted we stuck together.

Jason preceded me in both Little League and Babe Ruth League, smoothing the way. He was "Maas"; I was "Little Maas." His friends became mine. Then Jason went to California Polytechnic State University at San Luis Obispo, where he was a baseball all-American, and I opted for the University of California at Berkeley. But after college, both of us were drafted into the Yankee farm system.

That was the start of my four years in the minors. Jason was the leader, as usual, and sometimes when I'd see him moving ahead, I'd get rattled. In spring training at Fort Lauderdale in 1988, Jason moved up to a Class AA team. I was going to be left behind for another season of Class A ball.

"Jason, it's not fair!" I complained. "I *earned* a shot at Double A! I made the all-star team! What do they want? I don't know if I'm going back."

"Don't be hasty," he said. "Get away for a few days. Think about it. Talk to the Lord about it."

Jason and I often prayed and studied the Bible together, so we prayed about my situation. Jason asked God to impress on my heart what *He* wanted and to give me peace, whatever the decision would be.

Thanks to Jason I didn't walk away from the game. I returned to Class A ball. Within a month I had 12 home runs and was called up to the Class AA team—it hadn't taken long for Jason and me to be back together again.

The following season, 1989, I was sent to play in spring training with the Yankees. I got a pair of runs batted in against the New York Mets and opened eyes with a home run off Dwight Gooden. Nevertheless, I was sent to Columbus for my first season in the Class AAA league. Now I was the one who was moving ahead, but if Jason felt bad, he never let on. All he said was, "Show 'em, Kev."

And I did. I hit .320 and made the all-star team again that season. The manager switched me from first base, my usual position, to right field. Since Don Mattingly plays first for the Yankees, I figured they were thinking of me for the outfield.

Then everything began to go wrong. I came down with chicken pox and was out two weeks. Next I sprained my right knee in the outfield and missed another 10 days. Finally, in late July in a game at Indianapolis, I hit a hard line drive and was rounding first base when I had to put on the brakes. I felt my right knee pop. I went down in agony. I had a torn ligament that would require surgery. The doctors said they couldn't guarantee a thing. At the least, I'd be out for eight months.

Here I'd been so close to getting up into the majors, and suddenly my whole career was on the line. I was operated on in Lake Tahoe, Nevada, in August 1989. Jason was the first to call me after the surgery.

During the off-season of 1989-90, back home in Castro Valley, Jason ran with me and monitored my progress during agility drills.

I knew that Jason had his own problems, but he seemed to be more worried about mine. He had 113 hits and a .296 average, but management was contemplating sending him back to Double A for another season. "Well," he'd say philosophically, "at least I'll get a chance to play every day." And then in the next breath he'd ask, "How's the leg, Kev?"

"Feels good."

"Then why are you limping? Better take a break, give that new ligament time to take hold. There's no amount of leg and hamstring curls or running that will make it happen any faster. You can't rush nature."

As usual, Jason was right. Eventually, with prayer and patience, we *both* made it—I healed in eight months, and Jason and I both reported to the Columbus Clippers.

In May of 1990 I got on a hitting streak. In less than two months I had 13 home runs.

On the evening of June 28, the phone rang in my motel room. It was the Clippers manager, Rick Down. "Kev, you're going to New York in the morning," he said.

I'd made it at last. I was going to the majors. I was going to be a Yankee. All excited, I hurried to Jason's room. He was watching TV.

"I'm outta here," I blurted.

Jason looked at me. "No way . . . Are you serious?"

"Yeah . . . I am. Rick called. I'm going to New York. . . ."

Then it hit me: I was getting there before he did. I searched Jason's face for a hint of disappointment. But in the next instant my brother was out of bed, giving me a high five. "Congratulations, bro! You've worked *hard* for this! You deserve it!"

So here I was batting for the first time in Comiskey Park. I hit a weak pop-up to short, but later in the game I hit a line-drive single to right, and from there on out I just kind of relaxed. My rookie year with the Yankees had begun. By the time it was over, I would hit 21 home runs.

Now, as I begin my second season. I'm hoping—and praying— that Jason will be back with me soon. After all, we're a team, you know, and I'm only "Little Maas."

Dad Taught Me More Than Baseball
Mickey Mantle

(Written in 1953, while playing for the New York Yankees)

On April 17, 1953, I knocked a baseball out of Griffith Stadium in Washington, D.C. I'll not try and kid anybody by saying I didn't realize it was a long home run. My teammates beat my back black and blue and "atta boyed" me all over the place. They compared the drive with ones slugged by Babe Ruth, Lou Gehrig, Ted Williams, Joe DiMaggio and big people like that.

My folks back home in Commerce, Oklahoma, soon heard about it. When Mama telephoned that night, I gabbed first with her, then with my wife Merlyn, my three brothers, kid sister, and the neighbors who happened to drop in.

Frankly, I liked all these goings on, and there was no sleep in me that night. So I tuned in several sports programs, and they were talking about my homer. Then one announcer made me cry.

He mentioned my dad, Elven Charles "Mutt" Mantle.

This broadcaster recalled how my Dad taught me to hit both lefty and righty at the age of five, and how he raised me to become a professional ball player. What he didn't tell was how Dad tried to teach me to be a Big Leaguer off the diamond as well as on it.

While he was alive, I was Dad's life. Now, making good for Dad is my life. I guess that sounds a little strange, and maybe it is. Perhaps it may also sound strange that I still talk to "Mutt" Mantle, my father. That night in my hotel room I asked him:

"How about it? They say it went 565 feet."

Dad liked it but he wasn't satisfied. Now, don't get sore at him. He was just that way; he always demanded that I do better.

"It should have gone 600 feet," he said . . . inside me.

"Okay, okay, give me time," I said, and I'm sure he grinned.

I recalled when Dad drove me back home from Joplin, Mo., after I completed my first full year in the Class C Western Association. That was in September of 1950, and I was feeling pretty good for an 18-year-old. I batted .383, was plenty swelled up about it, and so began fishing for a compliment. "How about that .383 average, huh?"

Dad never took his eyes off the road. "You should have hit .400," he said. And I thought I saw him grin just a little then too.

Demanding better than good was Dad's way of telling me there's always a bigger Umpire than the man in blue on the field, and He's the real judge of what you do. My father tried to model my baseball techniques from the start as a writer works on a novel, or a composer on a symphony.

I was named Mickey Charles; Mickey after Mickey Cochrane, the great Philadelphia Athletics catcher, and Charles after my grandfather, Dad and Grandpa both played sandlot baseball.

According to Mama I was in the cradle when Dad asked her to make a baseball hat for me. When I was five he had her cut down his baseball pants and sew together my first uniform. He labored practically all his short life as a lead and zinc miner.

Anyway, I was five when he began teaching me how to switchhit. Dad was a left-hander; Grandpa, a right-hander. Every day after work they'd start a five-hour batting session.

Both would toss tennis balls at me in our front yard as hard as they could. I'd bat right-handed against Dad, and switch to left-handed against Grandpa. A grounder or pop-up was an out. A drive off the side of the house was a double, off the roof a triple, a homer when I hit over the house or somebody's window. I'm probably the only kid around who made his old man proud of him by breaking windows.

Dad hammered baseball into me for recreation, sure. But it was more than that. He was teaching me confidence by having unlimited faith in me. Dad was 35 and I was 15 when we played week-ends for the Spavinaw, Oklahoma, team. He pitched and I played shortstop.

Those games are the most cherished of my life. Bigger than any World Series. Why? Because we played together, and I watched

Dad's faith in action. He was never angry. He was always patient. He was unhappy when anybody made an error, even on the opposing team. He didn't try to outshine everybody else. He just tired to shine in himself.

In high school he wasn't happy about my playing basketball and football too. During a scrimmage one afternoon I got a kick in the left shin. I hardly noticed it, though I did limp home.

The next morning my leg was twice its normal size and discolored. There was no x-ray equipment in Commerce, so Dad borrowed the money, and got me to a specialist in Picher, Oklahoma. On the way I could see him sort of whispering to himself. He was praying.

The doctor diagnosed my trouble as osteomyelitis, a bad bone disease.

Dad borrowed up to his neck and hustled me to a clinic in Oklahoma City. There was even talk the leg would have to be amputated. When I thought it would make me give up baseball I almost went crazy. More for Dad's sake than mine. But Mama, Dad and Grandpa all hung on. They made me hang on.

Know what saved that leg? Prayer and penicillin.

When I got to recovering real good, I began swinging a sledgehammer at odd jobs and worked in the lead and zinc mines with Dad to put on weight and muscle. In a little over a year, I added eight inches and 40 pounds. One day in 1949, on the day I was graduated from high school, Dad said to me: "Get me a few hits for a graduation present." I sure tried, and I got him a single, double, and a homer.

Dad didn't tell me that a New York Yankee scout named Tom Greenwade was out there watching. After the game, I was signed first to the Independence, Kansas team, then to Joplin, both Yankee farm clubs. During the 1951 spring training season, I was brought up for a try-out with the Yankees!

Here was the chance to show everything Dad taught me. But how my teeth rattled! And how hard it was to control my anger. If I'd go without base hits for several days, I'd smash my knuckles against the concrete wall in the dugout, or hurt my toes kicking the water cooler. And after the game I'd ask Dad:

"What's the matter with me? What do I do wrong?"

"Bottle up your anger, boy," he'd say. "Let your bat do the talking for you." That's the way he always was. Gentle and patient.

I started the season as a right fielder for the Yankees. I'd flash sometimes, more often I fizzled. Then in a double-header at Boston I struck out five times in a row.

I cried like a baby. "Put someone in my place who can hit the ball," I blubbered to Manager Stengel.

Soon after this I was shipped back to Kansas City for more "seasoning." "I guess I don't have it as a Big Leaguer," I told Dad when I met him in Kansas City. "I belong in the minors."

First he whispered silently to himself, and then he said: "Mickey, things get tough at times and you must learn to take it. If that's all the guts you got, you don't belong in baseball."

His face was white and drawn. Dad had cancer, but I didn't know it.

He left. I stayed. I did some whispering too. On my knees. And I dug in. I got to hitting again. Before the season was out Mr. Stengel brought me back to the Yankees.

Seeing me start in the World Series was probably the proudest moment of Dad's life. In the second game I fell chasing a fly, ripped the ligaments in my right knee, and had to sit out the Series in a hospital bed. But it was all right. Dad was with me. He left a sick bed to see the Series.

"My back is acting up," he alibied, "but now I have to watch that knee of yours."

Then a doctor in the hospital told me Dad had cancer.

I guess I really woke up after Dad died. I mean I really got his message. Not because I had the responsibility and became the head of the family, looking after my mother and brothers and sister, and my wife. I guess I woke up to what he meant to teach me all the time. And I thank the Lord for Dad even though He did take him away at the age of 40.

There's been a Micky Mantle, Jr. around since last May. He doesn't know it, but he owns a ball, bat, and glove. It's all right with me if some more little Mantles come along in the future.

And some day I'm going to build a baseball park in Commerce, free to all, for every kid in town. It will be named Mutt Mantle Field, a sort of shrine for my father, who is still teaching me how to be a Big Leaguer—in the real sense.

 # To Forgive, and Forgive
Bill McCartney

Perhaps you've read about our 1989 football season at the University of Colorado, about the team that almost won the national championship, and about my being named Coach of the Year. You may also have read about my daughter, and the grandson she gave me. You might have seen photographs of that little boy, dressed in a miniature jersey with the number eight on it, the same number his father, the quarterback of our Colorado Buffaloes, once wore. And you probably saw pictures of the team with the quarterback's name, Sal, embroidered on their sleeves in dedication to him.

You'll know, then, that it was a season not only of victory, but of heartbreak as well. And for me, it was the culmination of more than a year of trials as I struggled with anger and held on to my faith in God, which was challenged more severely than it had ever been.

I first met Sal Aunese on a recruiting trip to southern California. He impressed me as a cocksure, determined quarterback who could outwit, outrun and outthrow his opponents. Sal was of Samoan background, powerfully built and taut, with an infectious, winsome smile. He had the versatility of a great player and the mark of a natural team leader.

"He's the one," I said to my assistants when I returned to Boulder, and, in fact, he was one of the best football decisions I ever made. Sal went into his first game as a sophomore substitute, and from then on he was my first-string quarterback.

As Sal's coach, I was obviously aware of his life outside the field house. Despite a demanding disciplinary code, a number of my players had been in trouble with the law off the field. Sal had been among them, and I suspended him from practice one spring because of an infraction.

When my wife, Lyndi, and I learned that our 19-year-old daughter, Kristy, was among the girls Sal was dating, I became concerned. If my daughter was going out with one of my players, the relationship could cause a conflict for me between my roles as a father and as a coach. But since Kristy was a freshman living her own life on campus, I decided not to interfere.

On a Saturday night in September 1988 as Lyndi and I were watching a film of that day's game, our third straight victory, Kristy appeared in the doorway looking tired and distraught. Suddenly she was standing behind us, blurting out, "I'm pregnant," and beginning to sob.

It's difficult for me to express the emotions that hit me at that moment, yet as we saw Kristy's pain, the first response Lyndi and I made was instinctively to turn to our daughter and hug her as she cried. Finally, quietly, I asked, "Who is the father?"

"Sal," Kristy said between sobs. "Sal Aunese."

We hugged her and told her we loved her, but even as I held Kristy in my arms, I could feel myself filling with anger. Sal was the boy I had recruited, coached, cared for. Somehow I felt betrayed.

To make matters worse, Sal, when confronted by Kristy's pregnancy, began to back away from her. Kristy felt confused and abandoned. Suddenly the conflict I had feared was now before me. As a father I resented Sal for rejecting Kristy and causing her so much pain; yet as a coach I had an obligation to hold our team together, and Sal was our key player, our leader. What was I to do?

The first thing I did was turn to the Lord. Over the years I had been open about my faith, ever since I had committed my life to Jesus Christ back in 1974. As Lyndi and I prayed now, it became clear to me what I had to do. Despite my feelings and the sense of betrayal, as a Christian I was obligated to forgive Sal.

When he finally entered my office several weeks later, Sal kept looking everywhere but directly at me. As he sat down, I silently prayed for the strength to battle with my own tangled emotions. "Sal," I began, "I want you to know, first of all, that Lyndi and I do not expect you to take responsibility for Kristy. We love her and will take care of her. But you do have a responsibility to the child, and someday you will have to decide whether you will accept your role as a father. Do you understand?"

" I understand, Coach," he said, his eyes glancing down at the floor.

Now came the tough part. "Sal," I said, "I want you to know that I forgive you. Lyndi forgives you. And we both still love you." His only response was a nod. Finally I said, "Your position on the team is not threatened."

When I finished, Sal nodded again, said, "Thanks, Coach," and left. He still had not looked at me.

I'd said the words, fulfilled my Christian duty, but almost every day I fought feelings of anger and frustration. Kristy moved back home from the dorm. Sal ignored her and dated other girls.

But on the field Sal Aunese led us through a fine season to finish 8-3, earning us an invitation to play Brigham Young University at the Freedom Bowl in Anaheim, California.

In Anaheim at the end of December, Sal was back on his home turf. His family and friends were there. Yet Sal did not have a good game. He didn't seem himself; he was slow to react. In the fourth quarter the score was tied 17-17, and we were missing one opportunity after another to get the ball into the end zone.

As I paced the sideline, I gritted my teeth and barked at the coaching staff. I had to make a decision: Hope for an eleventh-hour turnaround, or take Sal out of the game?

In desperation, I finally sent in a substitute for Sal. Then I watched in dismay as this replacement threw an interception. That set up a winning field goal, and we went down to defeat, 20-17.

I was thankful the season was over. By now Kristy was feeling increasingly isolated and lonely. Sal continued to pay little attention to her, and that hurt all of us. I prayed for him, but I found no peace. To forgive a person who has harmed you is one thing, but to forgive a person who has hurt someone you love is even harder. I reminded myself that I'd forgiven him, but I didn't feel it.

From friends, Kristy heard that Sal was not feeling well. Probably pneumonia, the doctors said. During spring vacation in March, just weeks before Kristy was to deliver, he checked in to a hospital for tests. Shortly afterward we got the devastating news. Sal had stomach cancer. It was inoperable; Sal had only months to live.

I rushed to the hospital to find a frightened Sal. "We'll help you through this," I promised.

In April Sal began chemotherapy treatments at almost the same time Kristy went in to have her baby. She named the boy Timothy Chase. Surprisingly, Sal showed up at the hospital and was among the first to hold him, but he still would not be reconciled to Kristy; another girl was constantly at his side. I ached for Kristy, and despite Sal's illness, my emotions regarding him were often in turmoil. I prayed for him and told God I forgave him again, but the anger kept coming back.

For the next couple of months Sal was in and out of the hospital; his face was drawn and his head was balding from the chemotherapy. By July he looked confused. His family came in from California, and I had long talks with Sal's sister, Ruta. She urged me to speak to Sal about his relationship with God.

At first Sal was unreceptive, and I found myself fumbling with words that led nowhere. Back home I prayed for him again and again, and about my seeming ineffectiveness now. "Lord, why can't I reach Sal?" I prayed. I thought about my anger. "Lord, take it away," I said. "I've forgiven Sal. Make that forgiveness real in my heart." The next time I visited him, Sal gave me a weak smile. I got right to the point. "Sal," I said, kneeling by his bed, "have you committed your life to Jesus Christ?"

He shook his head.

"Would you like to—right now?

"Yes," he said, tears in his eyes.

I took his hand, and together we prayed, Sal repeating the words after me. A great serenity came over him, and I silently thanked God for allowing me to set aside my feelings and play this role in Sal's life. And as I left the hospital, I became aware of something: The anger and resentment were gone; for the first time since Kristy's announcement back in September, I felt at peace.

Sal made it to our first three games of the 1989 season, which the team dedicated to him. He carried an oxygen support-system with him and sat in a private box. After each big play, his teammates would point to him in the stands.

Sal also now wanted to see Kristy and Timmy, and he spent some time with them during the week after our third game. He talked about what he wanted for his son.

Then on the next Saturday, our team's only open date of the season, Sal died. Kristy and Timmy were with him, and Lyndi and I were just outside in the hallway. The reconciliation was complete; Sal was at peace. After the funeral, Kristy and Timmy spent lots of time with the Aunese family, comforting one another; the joy of having Timmy around seemed to ease the Auneses' grief.

During the remainder of the season, the team felt Sal's presence. We played as a tight, unified group, winning game after game, ending the season with the Big Eight title, the number one spot in the national rankings, and an invitation to the Orange Bowl, which had been Sal's dream. Though we lost the bowl game to Notre Dame, we knew we'd had a golden season.

Now we're in a new football season, with all the hopes and challenges that go with it. Kristy and Timmy are living with us while she works and goes to college part-time. And Sal's memory constantly nudges me; I'm thankful for it. It reminds me that forgiveness is not based on feelings but on the act of forgiving. And when we act in faith, the feelings will follow.

 # Running with My God

Billy Mills

In the spring of 1974 I went back to Pine Ridge looking for answers. I stood on the dusty road that runs through the prairie town into the rolling Black Hills of South Dakota and squinted in the morning sun at the tiny ramshackle house where I'd spent the first 12 years of my life.

I had fought hard to leave the poverty of our reservation, and I had. Like other members of minority groups who make it outside their home turf, I was truly grateful for what I now had: a loving wife, three precious daughters and a comfortable home. Yet, like others, I still felt a restlessness at the core of my being. This had driven me here, back to my heritage, to look for something to ease the loneliness I was feeling.

This sleepy South Dakota town on the Pine Ridge Indian Reservation had not changed much in 20 years. The small board houses were still dwarfed by the wealth of nature surrounding them. I'd lived here with my mother, who was three-quarters French and one-quarter Indian; my father, a Lakota (Sioux) man; and my brothers and sisters and relatives. Sometimes we numbered as many as 15 in our four-room house. I hardly remember my mother, who died when I was small, but I can never forget my father, a stocky, muscular man with straight dark hair and a gentle, weathered face.

Dad had a fierce love for all of his children, but I felt there was a special connection between him and me. Now, standing in front of this small house, I pictured the year I was 12 years old. I saw the two of us as we walked home from church in the early morning: him broad-shouldered and proud in a dark tie and a white shirt, and me, a barely awake youngster in T-shirt and jeans. Since his stroke, he'd run a barbershop out of our house, and my favorite time of day was helping him set up for the day's business. I'd sweep the floor while he sharpened his shiny barber's scissors. And we'd talk. There wasn't anything I couldn't tell him.

All of us need to belong, yet even as a child I felt I didn't fit anywhere. "The white people don't want me," I'd complain to Dad. "To them I'm an Indian, and they have signs up in their town: 'No dogs or Indians allowed,' and they won't serve us in their restaurants. And my Lakota classmates, well. . ." I paused, embarrassed, "they say the only thing worse than a Wasicu [white man] is an Ieska [half blood]. I wish I was one thing or the other. But I'm nothing. I don't fit anywhere."

Dad never tried to placate me. Instead he'd try to find practical solutions for my feeling of not belonging. "Billy," he said to me more than once, "you can learn to be good at sports. It's a way to compete in white society." He must have seen the look on my face. We both knew I wasn't a natural athlete.

Or he would say, "It will be a struggle, son, to find a place in the white world—or to earn the respect of your father's people—but it is possible to walk in two worlds with one spirit. This, however, you must always remember: You are my son, and you belong. You belong to me."

I believed that I belonged to him and took strength from that knowledge. But that frail cord of acceptance snapped one morning several weeks later while Dad was cutting hair. He suffered another stroke and was taken to the hospital. That night when my sister told me he was dead, I ran out the creaking back door, over the hills, as far as my legs could carry me. I don't remember anything about the next two days.

But two things had changed: I now felt completely alone. And I'd started running.

I continued running at Haskell, one of the Indian boarding schools where my brothers and sisters and I were sent since there was no one at home to care for us. I would run five or ten miles on weekends, because it allowed me to get away from everybody else. And I just cried. I'd be crying while I was running. A half blood and an orphan—you couldn't feel much lonelier than that.

Before long, running, my means of escape, became my means of acceptance; I won a track scholarship to a predominantly white university. After graduation I earned a commission in the Marine Corps. Eventually, on October 14, 1964, the world was astounded at the Tokyo Olympics when I won the gold medal for the 10,000-meter race.

Dad had been right, that day 13 years earlier. Through sports I'd won acceptance and respect. The Lakota people gave me Warrior status and an Indian name, Makocé Terila ("Respects-the-Earth"). These were honors usually reserved for full-bloods. I'd married Pat, the woman I loved, who was white, and we settled in a beautiful community outside Sacramento, California. I had a good job selling insurance. I wanted to make sure that others wouldn't be left destitute because of a death, the way my own family had been. Things were going well. I should have been content.

So why was I standing here in front of this now-dilapidated house in Pine Ridge? I had thought that this long-sought acceptance would finally give me a sense of belonging. Instead there was a vacuum in the center of me. Was it that, even though two cultures accepted me, I knew I wasn't truly one or the other? *I* knew I didn't belong. Somehow I hoped that by coming back to my roots, back to where I was born, that I could find some answer to my restlessness. So Respects-the-Earth had come back.

As had happened before, when I first arrived at the reservation, I felt a fleeting sense of peace. At first I saw what I wanted to see: the ancestral land of a proud, strong people. So much of what I'd learned here was right: respect for the earth, for one's elders, for wisdom, for the culture of hundreds of generations now gone. But when my eyes adjusted, I saw the struggle of Pine Ridge: Once, we had been a people at home here. We had a spiritual grounding in this country and knew that the Black Hills was "the heart of everything there is." But promises had shattered, treaties had been broken. The Black Hills had been illegally taken away. Now the reservation meant inadequate housing, improper medical care, splintered families. The spirit of our people was imprisoned. There was poverty and despair.

Like other Lakota facing this struggle, I knew this place itself was not the answer to my heart's cry to belong.

I had come to the end of my resources. I needed someone wiser than myself. "Oh, Dad," I said, "you had such wisdom. Why aren't you here to tell me the secret of your serenity? How did you find peace in the face of need and ill health?"

Of course, Dad wasn't here. But another very wise man was— Fools Crow, an elder and spiritual leader of our tribe. I felt a new hope mixed with trepidation at the idea of an audience with him, but I knew I had to go.

While the honored citizens of many cultures have mansions and fancy cars, Fools Crow chose to live simply in a log cabin, miles from anywhere.

There was a tranquillity inside the small house. Fools Crow was past 70, his chestnut skin was weathered, but he still stood tall and his eyes shone with an ageless vitality. He received me and invited me to sit down. "I am troubled," I started. "There are questions to which I cannot find answers."

All of my frustrations came pouring out: my need to know where I truly belonged. How I'd looked everywhere and hoped to find my answer here. How the yearning still hadn't gone away.

"Billy," he started, speaking in Lakota, "I think you are still troubled that you are leska. But that is not the cause of your restlessness. Many of our people, full-bloods, go to the city as you did. Look what happens: Many of them drink, fight, become lost—lost souls. So they come back here, and what are they doing? Fighting, drinking. Their souls are lost here as well. The reservation is not the answer. A place does not give peace. So, what is the answer to this yearning?"

He paused and looked squarely at me. "The answer you seek lies with your Creator. Lakota, white, black; the Great Mysterious Creator made us all. There are two roads in life, the black road and the red road—the spiritual road. We are made with a yearning to walk the spirit road with our Creator. When you are on the spirit road, you may journey through any country in peace."

The burning in my chest told me he was right. This was his secret and this had been Dad's secret as well. God, the Great Mysterious Creator, had been Dad's strength, his center. This is why he had taken me to church, why he began each day in worship. Dad had counseled me to "walk in two worlds with one Spirit." Yet, I hadn't taken much time for God, for the "red road."

"Fools Crow," I said, "my father worshiped the Christian God. My daughters are in Catholic school. Am I turning my back on my heritage to worship this way?"

"Billy," he said gently, "there is one God. You honor your people in worshiping Him the way you know to be true."

A chilly wind parted the grasses as I left Fools Crow's cabin. But as I stood in the silence of the prairie, looking toward the Black Hills, I heard a familiar answer to my plea for acceptance, this time from a Father even greater than my own: *You are My son, and you belong. You belong to Me.*

I started down the dirt road. For the first time, I wasn't running away from, or toward, anything. I was running *with* my God, my Creator. And no matter where my earthly journey takes me, I know Billy Mills is already home.

 # Come Up Swinging
Dale Murphy

When the call came in November of 1983 from the office of the National League informing me that I had been named the league's most valuable player, I was surprised. Really. Sure I knew I was being considered; it was in all the papers. And yet, when I put the phone down, I didn't know quite what to think. It's a once-a-year honor that so very few players receive in their baseball careers. And now, I had been named MVP for the *second* straight year.

Throughout the rest of the day, with the telephone ringing and people slapping me on the back, do you know what I was thinking? I was thinking about 1977, the year I was 21, and the year that it looked as though I was finished with baseball forever.

I'd gone to spring training that season with great hopes. I knew I was on the verge of making it big; I was "the catcher of the future," or so people kept telling me—"the next Johnny Bench."

Try to imagine what it means to a young player, to be compared to a guy he'd admired and grown up watching on television and reading about in magazines. Since I was a boy in Portland, Oregon, I'd wanted to be a major-league catcher—like Bench, like Yogi Berra. Back home I was always playing ball, and when the American Legion team I played on in the summer finished third in a nationwide play-off, the Atlanta Braves signed me right out of high school. "A great defensive catcher with a live arm," was how they described me. They didn't point out that I wasn't much of a hitter.

In Kingsport, Tennessee; Greenwood, South Carolina; Savannah, Georgia; and on more road trips than I could count—three seasons altogether—I worked on that throwing arm every day, trying to make my dream come true, trying to make that arm carry me to the major leagues.

Then, at last, 1977. This was to be the year I made it to the big-time; at least, that's what everybody was predicting. Never mind the funny feeling I'd had throwing a few balls over the winter months; after all, the first couple of weeks of spring training were designed for getting the kinks out. I went south to the Braves' training camp ready to prove I was big-league material.

But there in West Palm Beach, Florida, something happened. Something that's still a mystery to me.

After a few weeks of warm-up training, we played our first intrasquad game. In the middle innings, I replaced the Braves' starting catcher. The first batter walked; and on the next pitch, he took off for second base. I jumped out of my crouch, and snapped a throw to catch him at second. The ball I threw sailed high over the second baseman's head and into center field. "Calm down!" I muttered to myself.

The next day, another freaky thing happened; I hit my own pitcher with a throw. And later, in base-stealing drills, I noticed that my throws were going awry more often than they were on target. *I'll settle down in a few days*, I told myself. *After all, throwing out basestealers is one of the things I do best.*

But another week passed, then two, and I didn't settle down. Every day something went wrong; throws I'd been able to make since junior high school were now something out of a horror show. I just couldn't make them. When anyone would ask me what was wrong, I'd just shrug my shoulders. All I knew was that, whatever it was, it was serious and I was in deep trouble. I began praying to God about it. Praying hard.

My arm felt good. The team doctors examined me a couple of times, had me pack the arm in ice after a couple of practices. But finally they had to admit that they couldn't find anything physically wrong, and they didn't know what to do. Every day, with the coaches and on my own, I reviewed and reviewed the fundamentals of throwing, what I had done before and what I was doing now. But the only thing that was different was that I couldn't make a good throw to second base anymore. And for a catcher there's no more important throw he can make; a catcher who can't throw to second is like a pitcher who can't get the ball in the strike zone.

Finally, a week before the start of the season, the Braves' manager called me into his office. "Dale, we're going to have to send you down to Richmond. You can work on your throwing there, and when you get things straightened out, we'll give you another look."

Richmond—back to the minors. Was I ever down as I began cleaning out my locker. Shoes, bats, gloves . . . I was nearly finished when I heard footsteps behind me. It was Paul Snyder, the Braves' assistant minor league director of player personnel.

"Sorry to hear you're leaving," he said.

"Yeah, Mr. Snyder, I am too. It's been a tough spring training."

"Dale, I just wanted to stop and tell you to hang in there. You're a healthy young guy, and you've got real baseball talent. You'll find your own way to fight back. I know I did."

For the first time all day, I at least felt good enough to smile, because I knew Paul understood as much as anyone how I felt. I'd gotten to know him pretty well during spring training. A couple of times he'd given me a ride to the ballpark from the players' quarters: one of those times he told me he'd just returned to work after suffering a pretty severe stroke. That really amazed me! He seemed just great. And he was, I learned, but only after he had completely retaught himself how to write, how to drive a car, and so on. You just have to recognize your weaknesses, he'd told me, and then take advantage of the things you're still able to do.

"Mr. Snyder, thanks for stopping by," I said, tossing my catcher's mitt into the duffel. "I appreciate it." What I didn't appreciate—or even realize—at the time was how important those few minutes would eventually be to me.

Because, when I got to Richmond, things didn't start getting better for me. Not the first week. Not the first month, or the second. Once in a while I'd throw a guy out trying to steal second base, just often enough to stay in the lineup. But every time an opposing runner would take off from first, my own pitchers would lie flat on the mound for fear I'd hit them with a throw.

Maybe if this had only been a slump, it wouldn't have seemed so bad. I'd been through slumps before; every baseball player has. You keep working hard, you keep the faith, and eventually you break out of it. But this wasn't just a slump, because it didn't go away.

I spent hours, at the field and in my tiny apartment, trying to find the flaw in my technique. Again and again I took the problem to God. Ever since a teammate of mine in Greenwood, Barry Bonnell, had led me to a new, deeper relationship with God, and a new church home. I felt close to Him. That closeness now gave me just enough confidence to go out on the field and keep my head up.

My teammates tried to cheer me up. They almost had to, because in the back of their minds they must have feared this strange thing that was happening to me as much as I did. If it happened to me— whatever it was—why couldn't it strike them next? Everybody tried to give me advice. "You're thinking about what you're doing too much. . . . You're not concentrating enough. . . . You're trying too hard. . . . You're. . . ." Pretty soon I was blocking out everything people told me.

"Hang in there, Dale," one well-meaning guy said to me one day. "You know, this kind of thing has happened to other players too. Remember Steve Blass of the . . . uh . . ." and then he knew he'd said the wrong thing.

No one needed to remind me of Steve Blass. He had led the Pirates to a World Series win over Baltimore six years earlier, in 1971, and pitched in the All-Star game the next season. And then, this top pitcher, in the prime of his career, lost his control, almost overnight. He simply could not get the ball over the plate. And no one knew by. By the 1974 season, at age 32, Blass was out of baseball. He never came back.

One night in Richmond I really had a bad game. My first throw to second went into center field, and by the time the game was over, the other team had swiped seven bases on me; only once did the second baseman even catch one of my throws. As I sat on the bench in front of my locker after the game, I could see my whole baseball career evaporating. Everything I'd worked hard for, dreamed about, lived for, was moving further and further out of my reach.

At last I had come to the point of thinking that maybe I should quit. I'd never be a catcher.

But as I sat there, I found myself thinking about Paul Snyder again. I could picture him driving me to practice. And I could hear what he was saying, too. *Life can deal you some tough blows, Dale. But it doesn't end. You can't wait for magic changes, for life to be just like it was before. You figure out what you still can do . . .* and then improve on that!

What I needed to do was reteach myself, just as Paul Snyder had done after his stroke. I had to do some retooling of my own. Okay, I wasn't going to make it as a catcher. That didn't mean I couldn't make it. What's it take to be a baseball player anyway? It's not only catching, but hitting and fielding and base-running and all the little intangibles that help build a group of individuals into a team. Oddly enough, my hitting so far that season had been better than it used to be. *Why not work on that?* I'd always had decent speed; *why can't I learn to read the pitcher's moves to help my own basestealing? Yeah, why not?*

I almost surprised myself with the fire of my thoughts. But it was true; life would go on. The question now was, would I go with it? Or quit? And deep down, I knew the answer. There was no way I was going to be drummed out of baseball without a fight.

The next day, I committed two more errors, but I also got two more slashing base hits. Two days after that, I collected the game-winning run-batted-in. I began stealing bases, sometime to set up runs. In short, I scratched and clawed the rest of that season, studying the game, the players, strategies, tactics. And it paid off. I had my best season ever at the plate: a .300 batting average with 90 RBIs. Suddenly, I began hearing other people talk about Dale Murphy as "a great offensive threat." That wasn't what I was before 1977, but I knew I was on my way to making a place for myself in baseball.

Seven seasons later, I think I've found that place. I flopped at first base when the Braves tried me there; my throwing just wasn't good enough. But then they moved me to the outfield, first to left and then to center, and with that little extra leeway allowed in throws from there, well, everything seemed to come together. My second year in center field, the Braves won the National League West title, and I received the MVP award. I also won a Gold Glove award that season—for best defensive play by a center fielder!

It's still a mystery to me, why one day I could make a perfect throw to second base and the next day I was so scatter-armed I never knew where the ball was going. Life is like that: Misfortune can be sudden, unexpected.

Baseball, I've found, is a lot like life itself. It's not so much a matter of how many times you're knocked down, but what you do when you get up. Maybe I do have two plaques that say, "Most Valuable Player." But I'm still a guy who couldn't make it as a catcher. I had to grab a bat and come up swinging.

Some Things Are More Important Than Winning
Joe Paterno

The Orange Bowl crowd let out a deafening roar. Penn State had just blocked a Kansas punt with a minute and 20 seconds left in the game. That gave us the ball at mid-field and a slim chance to get back in the game which we were losing, 14-7. Until then, it had looked as if our undefeated season of ten straight wins was going down the drain.

"You can do it!" our guys shouted at the offensive team as they surged onto the field. They believed it. But I had my doubts. Pepper Rogers, the University of Kansas coach, had done a great job with his team; if they could stop us for four more downs, the victory was theirs.

Then a 47-yard pass from Penn State quarterback Chuck Burkhart to Bobby Campbell put the ball on Kansas's three-yard line. Now the excitement really began to mount. Two plays later Burkhart ran around end for the touchdown. We now trailed, 14-13. With 15 seconds left, we had a big decision to make.

We could kick an almost sure extra point and earn a tie—we wouldn't win, but we wouldn't lose either. Or we could run a play from the three-yard line and try to win with a two-point conversion—we *could* win, but we could also lose if the play failed. It was win, lose or draw on this final play.

The stands were going wild and so, I guessed, were millions of fans watching on national television. But for me it was the game's easiest play to call.

"Let's go for two," I told Burkhart at the side line. Seconds later the teams were lined up. Now the possibilities for us were two—

win or lose. The play we chose was a rollout pass into the end zone. It was our best chance and we had it well rehearsed. But Kansas had scouted us even better, and their defenders batted away a Burkhart-to-Kwalick pass. Incomplete. The game was over. We had lost, 14-13, but I was satisfied that we had made the right choice.

Then someone yelled, "Penalty!"

"Kansas had twelve men on the field," one of my assistants screamed over the roar. The referee put the ball down one and a half yards from the goal and we got a second try. This time Campbell swept end and we won, unbelievably, 15-14.

Two totally different results, in just a matter of moments, yet both were completely acceptable to me. For actually we had done the same thing both times—we had played to win and done our best. And that was good enough for me. I'm a lot happier winning than I am losing. But to me winning is only the object of the game; it's not the *whole* game.

Winning is important. I don't like losing any better than anyone else. One time after a Penn State loss, my father-in-law, who is an architect, said to me, "Don't take it so hard, Joe. It's only a game."

"You're right," I answered. "But tell me, how would you feel if you designed a building and it fell down?"

Still, there are things more important than winning. What are they? Well, one is courage, not being afraid to lose. That's why I wanted the team to go for two points in the 1969 Orange Bowl—to win or lose with courage. Honesty and fair play are two more.

I'll never forget the time I learned about playing fair from Rip Engle, the coach I played under at Brown University and under whom I later served as an assistant coach at Penn State. Rip was another guy who didn't believe in the win-at-any-cost proposition.

In this case, we knew our Penn State team was in for a battle long before we took the field, and sure enough, our opponents took an early lead. Then midway through the second quarter one of our security men who walks the side lines with a walkie-talkie came up to me. "Hey, Joe," he said, "listen to this."

I put my ear to the receiver and could hear someone calling plays. "Check off; change to thirteen trap instead," the voice instructed. Out on the field I watched in disbelief. The quarterback stepped away from the center, switched signals and ran the play I'd heard on the walkie-talkie. The whole procedure was repeated on the next play.

"Coach," I said to Rip, "they're calling the plays from the press box. An assistant coach is telling the quarterback what to do with a walkie-talkie. The quarterback must have a receiver in his helmet."

"I can't believe they'd resort to something like that," Rip said, frowning. He knew as well as the rest of us that such a thing is against the rules. But when he held the walkie-talkie to his ear he learned the truth.

One assistant coach spoke up eagerly. "Now we can intercept their messages and signal defenses to the field in the second half," he said, rubbing his hands together. But Rip answered with a line I'll always remember. "I don't think I want to win that way," he said quietly.

And so we ignored the illegal electronics—and we did lose, but only on the scoreboard.

For me the excitement of football is in the anticipation, the hard work, the planning, the going all out, the playing with abandon, seeking the prize. That's where the exhilaration is; that's where the fun is.

I don't know who first impressed those ideas on me, but I suspect it was my dad. With three kids to feed and clothe and school, he and mama were sometimes hard pressed to make ends meet. Dad worked as a court clerk and usually spent his two-week vacation in a part-time job to earn some extra money. Mama helped too. I know she didn't go to the movies for many years in order to save the quarter it would cost.

Despite that kind of austerity, we were a happy family and Dad's attitude helped make it so. He didn't seem as concerned about the grades I got in a course as he was about my attitude toward learning. "Do you like the course, Joey?" he always wanted to know.

It was the same in sports. We lived in the Flatbush section of Brooklyn and I went to Brooklyn Prep. Sports were a big part of my growing-up years and Dad often would come out to see our football games. He was full of enthusiasm for the contest, the competition. He had had limited time for games as a child and was proud that his sons could play. He wanted us to enjoy the participation in sports.

Once we had a big game with St. Cecilia's of Englewood, New Jersey. That team was coached by a young man named Vince Lombardi who later went on to much bigger things in football. Both teams were undefeated, and we were leading, 14-13, when a 60-yard run by a St. Cecilia back late in the game ruined it for us. I was playing linebacker and I got my hands on him but he bounced off me and dashed past to make the winning touchdown. I felt miserable after the game—not just because we lost but also because I had missed that key tackle.

When Dad saw me later, he never mentioned that crucial miss. "It was a good game, and I was proud of you, Joey," was all he said. Winning—and worrying about winning—wasn't everything to him.

Our problems in college football have become more complex as interest in the game has grown. The football program at some colleges has entered the world of high finance, with tremendous emphasis on achievement on the football field. To win, a college needs good athletes, and so outstanding high school players all over the country are courted. Some overly ambitious recruiters break the rules and offer an athlete a lot more than a scholarship, room and board. It's the same thing as a businessman making pay-offs or a public official accepting them, and some people in football are playing the same winning-is-everything kind of game.

Even so, it's gratifying to me that there are so many athletes today who are turned off by offers of extra money, wardrobes and cars. Those young men still want to play according to the rules; winning special favors isn't as important to them as playing it straight and clean.

Once I really had to decide what was important about football. The New England Patriots of the National Football League were looking for a new head coach and they offered me an extremely rich contract. It represented a fortune to me. My wife Sue and I did a lot of soul-searching and I lost more than a little sleep before making my decision. When I finally turned the job down, I did so, I think, because I consider myself more than a football coach. I'm also a teacher and I want to work with young people.

When the news got out, many people were surprised, but I didn't think it was out of character for me. I declined because I seriously doubt that I would be happy coaching professional football. There, I believe, the emphasis is entirely on winning. But for me, concentrating only on winning would soon take the fun out of football.

If I have any success to claim, it lies in the fact that I love what I am doing. Because I do, I can go home to my family at night and relax, and after Sue and I have had a family prayer with our five children and have tucked them in, I can sleep like a log knowing I've got something worthwhile and fun to do the next day.

That's what's important to me.

 # An Unlikely Champion
Calvin Peete

My friends used to laugh when I told them that, one day, I was going to win a professional golf tournament.

"Calvin," they said, "poor, black guys who drop out of school to work in the vegetable fields don't play professional golf. Neither do guys who didn't even hit their first golf ball until they were twenty-three. You can't even straighten your left arm, and everybody knows that in golf, you have to keep that left arm straight. Calvin, you won't ever be a pro golfer."

I remember giving those friends a wry smile and telling them that I'd find a way. That was 18 years ago. And since then, I've done exactly what I said I was going to do. Most people say I've succeeded in spite of my background; I say I've made it because of it.

We never had much money when I was growing up in the farmlands of central Florida—vegetable pickers never did. You'd be out from 5:30 in the morning until the sun went down, and if it had been a good day, you might make $10. Ten dollars, eight dollars, five, it didn't matter; we desperately needed every penny we could get. That's why I dropped out of school in the eighth grade; it meant another pair of hands in the field making money.

I was always dreaming, though, that there was more for me, that I had a future beyond the next row of beans. My father must have known what I was thinking those times he caught me wistfully looking into the sky. "Son," he'd say, "God has a plan for your life. One of these days you'll find out what it is, and when you do, make sure you work hard to make that plan go places."

Eventually, I got out of the fields, first as a peddler, from Florida to upstate New York, to the migrant farm workers and then as a manager for some apartment buildings in Fort Lauderdale. For a while I wondered if this could be the plan my father talked about.

And then it happened. I was in upstate New York. All that week, some of my friends had been badgering me to play golf with them, and I kept turning them down. They'd been caddies when they were younger; I guess that's why they found more pleasure in chasing a little white ball around in the hot sun than I did.

One day they told me we were all going out to eat but, instead, drove to the golf course. "Calvin," they said, "you can either come play golf with us or sit here in the car until we're finished."

It was 95 degrees that day. *Anything* was better than sitting in that hot parking lot.

Just a couple of days later, I had myself a secondhand set of golf clubs and a book by Sam Snead on how to play the game, determined that I was going to become a golfer. I guess you could say I'd been hooked. From the moment I first stepped up to the tee, I loved the game; it had felt so natural, so much a part of me. I couldn't think of anything I'd rather be doing. And in my heart, I felt certain that now I had found that plan God had for me. What had Dad said? "When you find out what God's plan is, you'll have to work hard to make it go." Then that's what I'd have to do with my golf game.

First day back in Fort Lauderdale, I dragged out my "new" clubs, took a shag bag filled with some old balls I'd picked up, and headed over to the public park. I found a grassy spot at one end, chose a target about 100 yards away and aimed every one of my shots to that one spot. Fifty shots, retrieve. Fifty shots, retrieve. I didn't go home that night until it was too dark to see.

I was my own teacher. I didn't dare take a lesson for fear the instructor would tell me I didn't have a chance at being a top-flight golfer, what with my late start and bad arm and all. So I just kept hitting and hitting on my own, month after month. I even figured out a way to rig up a motor-driven camera, mounted on a tripod, so I could take sequence pictures of my swing and study them later. I devoured any book on golf I could find, books by greats like Ben Hogan and Jack Nicklaus and Bob Toski and Doug Ford.

Another time, when I was at the local sporting goods store looking to buy a new golf glove, I learned from the salesman that I had been gripping my clubs all wrong. "That's why your hands are so raw and blistered," he told me. I bought the glove, went right back out to the park and, under the dim light of the streetlamps, tried out the new grip. That was the night the police drove up to find out what I was doing there at that hour. I'm sure my wife Christine, whom I'd recently married, must have thought I was as crazy as those two officers did.

Of course, there was still the matter of that left arm of mine. Read any book on golf and it will tell you: Keep the left arm straight as you swing through the ball or you'll spray shots all over the course. Well, there was no way I could keep my left arm straight gripping a golf club, or anytime for that matter. I had fallen out of a tree when I was 12 and broken my elbow in three places. It healed eventually, but left me with a permanent bend in that arm. But in all those practice sessions I discovered something no book ever said: That by lining up my body with the greatest care and setting up the shot in my mind—just as I used to do in the pool hall—I could use a shorter, more compact swing with just as great accuracy and just a little bit less distance, than with a full, by-the-book swing.

Within six months after my initiation into golf, I shot below 80; a year and a half, and I had broken par. And I was convinced that I really had found my niche, my thing to do in life. I joined the mini-tour (the minor leagues of golf) in Florida in 1972 and after three tries at earning my qualifying card for the big tour (and so many hours of practice that I hate to even think about it), I finally qualified in 1975. At 32, I was the oldest rookie on the PGA tour. But I'd made it, the poor black kid from the vegetable fields of Florida. One of my first seasons, I made it to the final round of the United States Open, and do you know who my playing partner was?—the great Jack Nicklaus.

But for all those moments of excitement the first three years, the day-to-day realities were proving much more harsh. Very simply, I was barely surviving. There was a 25th place finish here and a 30th place there, but for all my scrimping and saving on low-cost motels and a beat-up car to get me and my caddie from tournament to tournament, I just wasn't making it. If it hadn't been for Christine, at home, teaching school, we would have gone broke.

And that was really getting me down. I'd been so sure when I seriously took up golf that I was doing what God wanted me to do. I'd worked hard; I'd made the tour. And then, the bottom fell out. I was going bust and it was driving me up the wall. Every tournament there was some new disappointment. It had me thinking, hard. *Had I been mistaken all along? Had I somehow missed God's leading?* Maybe my friends had been right all along. I didn't want to believe that; but my scores were forcing me to.

"Christine," I said one night, "this may sound funny to you, but I kind of feel like Job. How could God have brought me so far, only to let me down like this?"

"Calvin, did you ever think that it might not be God letting you down at all," Christine said. "Maybe you're letting yourself down."

"What do you mean?" I said.

"Well, where's that camera you used to take pictures of your swing?"

"In the closet, but . . ."

"And your shag bag?"

"In the basement. But I go to the driving range now."

"How about your putting? How long are you working on that each day? Calvin, we're all awful proud that you made it on the tour. But I think since you have, you've gotten out of the habit of working at your game, or really studying yourself, like you used to do. You're practicing . . . but you're not working."

I wanted to say I'd paid my dues, that tour players didn't need to hit balls from dawn till dusk in a city park with just a shag bag and a nine iron. But I knew Christine was right. Once I had made the tour, I'd gotten away from that recipe I'd learned from my father. God's plan never changed; He never gave up on me. I was the one who had given up on hard work and determination.

When the 1979 PGA tour opened in Arizona the following January, I was still at home, armed with a new movie camera and a full shag bag. I went back to those long, grueling days, to hours working to perfect just one difficult shot. It was slow, tough medicine; but it was the only way.

I joined the tour again when it came to Florida in mid-March, and by June I could sense all the work beginning to pay off. I tied for 11th place in the U.S. Open, and just a month later, put together four straight rounds in the 60s, closing with a 65 to win the 1979 Greater Milwaukee Open by five strokes. That was my first tournament victory ever. Three years later, I won in Milwaukee again on my way to being the fourth winningest golfer on the tour that year.

It's been a long road from the fields to the fairways, one a lot of people said was impossible from the beginning. But you see, I knew something maybe they didn't: That God had a plan for me—but I had to be willing to work at it. When you work hard and pray hard you have a combination that can take you places you've never imagined.

It's taken me from green beans to a putting green . . . and far, far beyond.

 # Ten Words I Never Forgot
Cathy Rigby

The woman was a famous movie star. She had come to visit her daughter at the summer gymnastics camp for girls that my husband and I run near Fresno, California. When the time came for the daily workouts, the actress watched her daughter from the sidelines. The girl was good, though not good enough to ever compete at a championship level. And I noticed, today, how nervous she was.

When the girl finished, her mother called out: "That was awful. You looked like a sack of potatoes tumbling downhill." The girl burst into tears. My heart went out to her.

I found myself remembering the day one of my own gymnastic performances put me close to tears. I might have gone ahead and shed them, except for something my mother said to me then.

When my mother was carrying her first child, she was stricken with polio, and she has been confined to a wheelchair and crutches ever since. But she never let that discourage her. She managed to raise five children and have a career as well.

One day I decided to join a gymnastics program at a nearby park. Before long, I was totally absorbed in it. By 1972, I was on the U.S. Women's Gymnastics Team for the Olympic Games in Munich. I couldn't think of anything else but winning a gold medal.

It had become my habit, during practice sessions and the warm-ups before a contest, to pray—asking God for the strength and the control to get through the routine. That day in Munich, I was tense with the determination not to disgrace my country and myself. But, though I competed to the best of my ability, I didn't win a gold medal. I was crushed. After the winners were announced, I joined my parents in the stands, all set for a big cry. I managed a faltering, "I'm sorry. I did my best."

"You know that, and I know that," my mother said, "and I'm sure God knows that, too." She smiled and said ten words that I never forgot: "Doing your best is more important than being *the* best."

Suddenly I understood my mother better than ever before. She had never let her handicap prevent her from always doing her best.

Now I went over to the sobbing girl and put an arm around her. "Honey," I said, "I've been watching you improve all summer and I know you have done your best, and doing your best is more important than being the best. I'm proud of you."

She smiled at me through her tears. Maybe somewhere, someday, she'll pass those words along.

 # Moving On

Stacey Robinson

The smell of smoldering leaves fills this quiet neighborhood as the kids on my block peel off their New York Giants sweatshirts and play a fast pickup game of touch in front of my house. It is autumn and, above all, football season. That means something extra to me because that is what I am—or was. A professional football player. I'm not in uniform this year.

It feels a bit strange sitting here and not worrying about how I'll face across the line of scrimmage come Sunday afternoon, or the intricately timed pass patterns I'll run as a wide receiver for the New York Giants. The last game I played was January 27, 1991—the Super Bowl in Tampa against the Buffalo Bills. I have a champion's ring on my right hand to show for it.

Though I'm only 29, it's time to move on. I'll miss the game, but I won't miss the uncertainty, from year to year, of whether I'll have my job back in the starting lineup or if I'll be cut loose. More than once I was let go just as the season began. Those were hard times. But they taught me something.

Everyone knows how competitive the National Football League is. What most people aren't aware of is the intense level of competition *within* a team. Your job is always up for grabs. Someone younger, faster or bigger comes along and you're on the bench. Or off the team. That's just the way it works.

Things really get serious in late-summer training camp. Camp can be fun—the anticipation of a new campaign, the media coverage, seeing old friends—but it can also be brutal. You practice in 90-degree temperatures in full gear, chugging Gatorade so you don't dehydrate, and gasping in an oxygen mask after the coaches put you through relentless sets of wind sprints. There are blocking drills and scrimmages, stretching exercises and weights. My body never ached more than after the first week of camp. But it's a good ache, the kind that says you've worked hard. The one cushy thing is that they feed you abundantly—plenty of pasta and steak.

The coaching staff scrutinizes players, finds out who's got stronger in the off-season, who's lost a step off the line, whose injury isn't mending. Sometimes a single play in an exhibition game makes all the difference. For many players the pressure is greater than the play-offs.

Last year the Giants camp—the year that was to become a championship one for us—I had my typical preseason. I started strong, running crisp pass patterns and snagging balls thrown by quarterback Phil Simms and backup Jeff Hostetler. I was sure I'd start the year on the roster, unlike '89 when I was cut loose until one of the other receivers went down with an injury in midseason. I'd survived two roster cuts already. Then one day on a simple post pattern, something popped in my leg. I'd pulled a groin muscle, a pesky injury than can keep you out a week or an entire season. It always seemed to happen to me.

Suddenly my confidence wobbled. One last roster cut remained before the season opened. Had I impressed the coaches enough? I got an inkling of what they were thinking during a rowdy locker-room meeting with Head Coach Bill Parcells. "William Roberts, stand up!" Parcells shouted. "William's having a *great* training camp! Pepper Johnson, stand up! Here's another guy having a great, great camp! Let's hear it for Pepper! And Stacey Robinson! Stacey *was* having a great camp until he went down the tubes with a groin."

Coach caught my eye just as he moved on to the next Giant to be exhorted. Shucks, I knew my injury problems had always irked him. A bad hand kept me out 12 weeks during my rookie year in '85; early in '86 Ronnie Lott and the San Francisco 49er secondary clobbered me as I caught a pass over the middle, fracturing my jaw. I'd spent my share of time on the injured reserve. And now this. I was disgusted.

I slept poorly the rest of August. There were a couple of hot rookie receivers showing their stuff in camp. I kept imagining the final roster and my name not on it. I'd be back at square one again! Finally the list went up. I scarcely breathed as I scanned it. Near the bottom I saw ROBINSON, S.—WIDE RECEIVER. I went to my locker to say a relieved prayer of thanks. My feet were barely touching the ground, as if I was about to pull in one of Phil's pinpoint sideline passes on a two-minute drill.

The euphoria lasted all of two days. Then during afternoon practice, Coach Parcells signaled me to come with him. The clink of my cleats on the concrete runway leading to the deserted locker room seemed to echo throughout immense Giants stadium, a place that would be packed with 77,000 roaring fans come Sunday. I wanted to be able to run out of this tunnel and have those cheers fill my ears. Instead I felt like a man going to the gallows. When the coach calls you off the field for a private chat it's rarely good news.

"Stace," Parcells began, planting himself in front of my stall, "Marshall and Taylor are ending their contract holdout. They're coming back for the opener." He didn't have to say more. I knew they needed to free up room on the roster for the two stars. I'd have to go. "Trust me," he continued. "You'll be back. Just like in '88 and '89. I promise."

I shook my head. I tried to speak. Nothing. *Cut again.* Third year in a row. This time it seemed so final.

"Maybe if you hadn't injured yourself again . . ." His voice faded out. Careers are full of ifs. Maybe it was my injury, or the way I juked on a certain pass pattern, or a particular ball I dropped once but another guy never missed. You just don't know. He slapped me on the knee and walked off. The cool, moist air bore the familiar smells of sweat, towels and talc. I drew it in deeply, wondering if this was the last I'd see of an NFL locker room. Then I cleared out my stuff before the others came off the field.

That night I got a call from Dave Bratton, our team chaplain. Good old Dave. He'd always stood by me at these hard times. The next day we had what was by now becoming our traditional farewell breakfast (Dave always bought). The color drained from his face when I pressed my head into his shoulder and sobbed. But when he began patting my arm, I looked up and smiled slyly. "Gotcha!" I laughed.

I knew that making a joke out of it would help Dave feel better about my leaving. Besides, I couldn't let this make me crazy as it had in past years. As much as I would miss suiting up on Sundays, I would miss just as much leading our team chapel meeting on game mornings. I mentioned that to Dave and he said, "You know, coaches and owners think they are completely in charge of what happens. But we know different, don't we? You'll be back again."

Back or not, it began to sink in that I had to start thinking about my future. When I'd been cut before, I did like most players; I stayed in shape and kept my options open. It's hard to forget about football. Sportswriters are fond of using the analogy that football is a microcosm of life. Sometimes, though, the people in pro football act as if life is a microcosm of football. They lose sight of reality. When players leave the game, often they don't know what to do with their lives.

I'd watched it happen to ex-players; I didn't want it happening to me. In previous years I'd gone back to college, taking courses toward a masters of business administration degree. I enrolled again. Still I could not completely shake my sense of failure. I'd really thought this was my year. I began to feel that even if they asked me back I'd refuse. You can take just so much.

Finally one night I picked up the phone and had a long talk with my mom back in Minnesota. I turned to Mom when things got really tough. I poured out my troubles. "Mom, I can't concentrate on anything."

"Look, Son," she said, "you know what you've got to do. Have you been reading your Bible?"

Sheepishly I admitted that my study time had slipped.

"Stacey, you've got to get back to the Word! That's where you'll find the direction you need."

I got off the phone and grabbed my Bible. I flipped it open to a familiar passage: "Consider it pure joy, my brothers, whenever you face trials . . . because you know that the testing of your faith develops perseverance" (James 1:2, 3, NIV).

That word, *perseverance*. It hit home. Isn't that what we all need? In our faith? In our work? The worst mistake I could make, I realized, was not to get on with things.

So I did. And soon enough the Giants called. My friend Odessa Turner had broken his collarbone. Parcells wanted me back. I didn't say yes. I thought about it. I prayed. I talked to Mom. I stayed close to the Word. Then I said yes.

I went on to have a good year, a great play-off and a role in the Super Bowl. It's the second Super Bowl ring I've got (the first was in '87). I've had a good career. But this season I didn't want to go back to camp and fight all over again for my position. It was time to finish my MBA and look to the future.

Sometimes the future is a scary thing, especially for men who've been paid to play little boys' games. But I know one thing is certain about the future—God will be there, as He is every day of our lives. When we stay close to the Word, He guides us along the way.

 # Something More
Mike Schmidt

The best and the worst year of my life started with a telephone call. From that moment on, a whole series of strange things went into motion; I haven't been the same person since.

The call came just after baseball season ended in the fall of 1977. Andre Thornton was on the line. "How about getting together sometime?" he said. I was surprised to hear from him. Andy was the first baseman for the Cleveland Indians—a real first-class fellow. We'd been in the minors together, but now we were playing in different leagues, and I hadn't seen much of him. I did remember seeing him at batting practice one day the year before, when he'd come around the batting cage to talk to me. The unusual glow on his face that day sort of stuck in my mind.

I learned the reason for Andy's call a week later when he and his wife, Gert, came to dinner with Donna and me at our house in Cherry Hill, New Jersey. Andy was a very religious man, something I was not, and he'd seen something in one of the sports columns where I'd mentioned God. Well, the press is always putting words into players' mouths and I couldn't remember having said anything about God to any reporter.

It was true that recently I had started dropping into Baseball Chapel before the game on Sundays. Maybe that's how the item got in the sports column. However, the weird thing about it was that I *had* been doing some thinking that you might call "spiritual." Something was happening to me; something was making me feel uneasy. As we sat down to dinner I wondered if Andy had sensed that.

Actually, things were going so well for me in those days that it seemed silly to feel uneasy. My life had been charmed ever since college when I was all-American in baseball at Ohio University. The Phillies had drafted me in 1971, and except for a rotten rookie year, my career had been on a steady upswing. I'd been the National League's home-run leader in '74, '75 and '76, and I knew I was on my way to becoming the highest-paid player in the league. Still, I couldn't forget the afternoon a few weeks back when I was outside our house casually shooting baskets in the driveway hoop. There was a moment when I looked over at the Mercedes and Corvette parked there. Out back was our swimming pool; inside the house, my beautiful Donna was busy in the kitchen. *What did I do to deserve all this?* I said to myself. *Why am I so blessed?* It's a strange thing to say, but success was bothering me.

We had a good time that night, two baseball players and our wives sharing a meal and lively talk. Gradually the conversation turned serious, and Andy brought up some of the very things that had been on *my* mind, such as why we should have been singled out for baseball stardom, and what it all meant: the prestige, the money, the sports cars, the mansions. It didn't surprise me that Andy related everything to faith in God, and I was impressed with his knowledge of the Bible, yet the memorable part of the evening was still to come. We turned to the subject of families.

Gert and Andy began telling us about their two children, little Theresa and Andy Junior. From across the table Donna and I looked at each other. We each knew what the other was thinking. "Well," I said out loud, "we talk about having it all, but there's one thing Donna and I don't have, something we've been denied—a child."

Andy Thornton was very moved by this, and right then and there, while we were still at the table, he said a prayer for us. In simple, direct, beautiful words he asked God to give Donna and me patience and understanding—and a child of our own.

The evening came to a close. Gert and Andy climbed into their van, waved good-bye and drove away.

One week later Gert and Andy were riding in that same van with their two children. There was a sleet storm. The van skidded and crashed. Andy and their son escaped with minor injuries. Gert and their daughter were killed.

And one week after that Donna learned she was pregnant.

This was just the start of that best, and worst, year of my life. The grace with which Andy met and survived his heartbreak inspired everyone in baseball, and the public as well. It led me to think deeply about the kind of faith Andy had. I pictured again the glow I'd seen on his face the day he'd called me over by the batting cage. I remembered now how he'd told me about his having given "the reins" of his life to Christ. I thought, at the time, he'd gone off the deep end.

The winter set in. Donna was doing well. But I was still wrestling with my own uneasy thoughts about life, when I happened to come across a calling card in my wallet. It read: Dr. Wendell Kempton, President of the Association of Baptists for World Evangelism.

Kempton had been a speaker at one of those Sunday Baseball Chapels and he'd talked about having been a heavy drinker, "a real party animal," before his conversion. I'd been impressed by his dynamism. Now I didn't even telephone; I drove right to his office in New Jersey. When he seemed pleased to see me, I sat down and said, "Can we just talk?"

Before I left his office, Wendell suggested getting together for dinner and a short session of Bible study at his house. "Why not bring your wife along?" he said. "And any players who might want to come."

Some "short session"! What was supposed to be a half-hour Bible lesson turned into a six-hour marathon in which Wendell traced God's plan of salvation from Genesis through Revelation. We were spellbound. In awe. And so eager to hear more that we decided to meet again in 10 days, this time at any house.

By the things were really churning inside me. *Am I living for the Corvette and Mercedes out there in the driveway?* I asked myself. *There has to be something more.*

Alone in our bedroom one day, I came across a pamphlet, a tract, with something on it called "The Sinner's Prayer." I started to read it, then I began to say the words out loud, then little by little those words became my words. I acknowledged my flaws. I acknowledged my need of Jesus. I asked Him to come into my life and be my personal Savior.

At our next Bible class, which six other players and their wives attended, I told everyone what had happened. The group was stunned. Yet when I described what it was like to turn over the reins to Jesus, I think no one thought I'd gone off the deep end.

Spring came, Donna was plump and happy. Together we signed up for some natural-childbirth classes. By the time I went to spring training in Clearwater, I was feeling great. I could tell that this was going to be my best year so far.

How wrong can a guy be?

First I bruised my ribs and was on the disabled list for a month. Things went downhill from there. Out of 513 at-bats that year, I got only 129 hits. I struck out 103 times. My batting average was an anemic .251. The press got on my back. The "boo-birds" in the stands never let up. The harder I tried, the worse things got.

"What's this all about?" I asked Wendell Kempton in desperation. "I become a Christian and this is what happens?"

Wendell was patient with me. He knew that eventually I'd understand that being a Christian did not guarantee clear sailing all the time. And he counted on my remembering that I, after all, was the baseball player who had put the worship of God above "success." Meanwhile Wendell gave me some advice that helped relieve the pressure.

"Mike," he suggested, "when you come to bat, tell the Lord outright that you're going to give Him 100 percent. If you strike out, you'll strike out doing your best. If you get a hit, that'll be doing your best too. Put the outcome in His hands."

I tried it. It was tough at first, when the "fans" were screaming for my blood and the negative thoughts crowded in. *Oh . . . I'm oh for four*, I'd think. *Fifty thousand people are expecting me to DO something*.

Then I'd pray, *Lord, clear my mind. Let Your will be done*.

It helped. It helped me get through the season, which, as it turned out, was truly the worst year in baseball I ever had.

But then, it was the best year too, because of Jessica. I was there in the hospital, suited up like a doctor in a gown and mask, watching as my daughter was born. Within minutes, they placed her in my hands. I remember noticing a fleck of crimson on her tiny cheek, where the scalpel had lightly scratched her. Today Jessica is a pretty girl of nine, and that scar is so minuscule that you can see it only if you're looking for it. But it's very dear to me because it reminds me of that wonderful moment when I first held her and everything on earth and in heaven fell into place.

In that unforgettable moment I knew for certain that life wasn't about money or status or cars, or even baseball stardom. To this day I know it's about things like loving God, serving others; it's about families and husbands and wives loving and respecting one another; it's about having kids to raise and love.

Don't get me wrong; my baseball career is still very important to me. But nowadays I can get a home-run feeling just walking my kids (yes, we have two, the second one six-year-old Jonathan) to the school bus in the morning, or playing a game of golf, or hugging Donna, or telling someone about Jesus.

The simple things—they can give you a home-run feeling too.

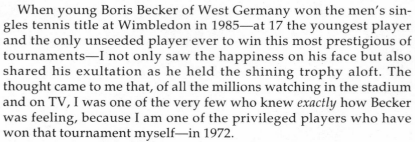

More Than One Way to Win
Stan Smith

When young Boris Becker of West Germany won the men's singles tennis title at Wimbledon in 1985—at 17 the youngest player and the only unseeded player ever to win this most prestigious of tournaments—I not only saw the happiness on his face but also shared his exultation as he held the shining trophy aloft. The thought came to me that, of all the millions watching in the stadium and on TV, I was one of the very few who knew *exactly* how Becker was feeling, because I am one of the privileged players who have won that tournament myself—in 1972.

Now, at age 39, I'm still playing tennis, but a lot of my time is spent teaching eager youngsters the fundamentals of the game. I also try to teach them Christian values, because Jesus Christ came into my life when I was still in college in California, and that has given me a peace and a purpose that has made all the difference ever since.

It's easy to see how youngsters can become confused these days, or pick up the wrong values. Sports have become big business, with enormous sums of money paid to first-class athletes. As you work your way toward the top, the pressure and ego temptations become greater. It's easy to be jealous of other athletes who are more successful. I tell my tennis students, "Can you conceive of Jesus being jealous of the rich young man who came to Him for advice? Or envious of John the Baptist because at first John was better known than He was?"

Another confusing thing for some of the kids is that Christianity stresses unselfishness and going the extra mile for others. But competitive sports emphasize winning, and in tennis—which is often a one-on-one duel to victory or defeat—this direct confrontation can be ferocious. My advice is play hard, play fair and respect your opponent while you're doing your best to overcome him or her.

There are seven principles that I teach, principles just as applicable to life as to tennis. The first is, set high goals. The higher you set the bars for yourself, the higher you're likely to jump.

The second is, prepare as thoroughly as you can. No worthwhile goal in sports is ever achieved without paying the price of preparation. That means practice—endless, exhausting practice; taking care of your body; driving yourself to the limits of your endurance, mental and physical.

I remember when I was moving up in the tennis world. I used to imagine myself in the finals at Wimbledon. In this fantasy I was always in the fifth set of a grueling match against a brilliant and tenacious opponent. Game stood at five all. Tennis talent on both sides of the net was about equal. The man with the last ounce of stamina and determination—in other words the *best-prepared* player—was going to win. And the day came in 1972 when I *did* find myself in the finals at Wimbledon, playing in the fifth set against Ilie Nastase of Romania. And I won—just barely—possibly because I was a fraction better prepared than he was.

The third thing I tell young players is, never give in to discouragement. There have been some sensational comebacks in the history of tennis, but never by a player who gave up.

The fourth is, strive for self-control. If you blow your top, you're likely to blow the match along with it because you'll lose your concentration and you may not get it back.

Rod Laver, the Australian player whom I consider the greatest of all, knew this, and I never knew him to let his temper get out of hand. It's a hard lesson for a fiery, competitive youngster to learn, but it's really a matter of self-interest. If you lose your self-control, you aren't hurting the linesman, or the umpire, or your opponent. You're hurting yourself.

Here's the fifth thing I say to young players: Go for absolute honesty. When you're starting out in tennis, almost all your matches will be played without linesmen or umpires. You will have to call the close shots, because your opponent can't see them. Now and then there may be a temptation to call one out when you know it was in. Don't do it. You'll have to make up your mind very early not to cheat; otherwise one little deception will lead to another, and first thing you know, your self-respect—and perhaps your reputation—is down the drain. You can't carry that kind of burden if you want to be really good.

My sixth suggestion is, choose a good role model for your life. Someone to look up to, to admire, someone who represents good values. I tell them that my own role model is Jesus, and I think they can't do any better than that. "Having Christ as a role model," I tell them, "doesn't mean you have to be a pushover. Christ faced tough decisions. He came through tough situations. He never complained. He never whined. He just did what He knew was right with a combination of love and strength and courage that has never been equaled."

Finally, I say to the kids, "Look for God's purpose in your life." If they reply, "How do I do that?" I tell them to watch for the talent in their makeup. Everyone has a talent for something, and this is God's gift. He plants it in us; then it's our job to make it grow.

"Once you've recognized your chief area of talent," I say to young players, "once you've decided that it's a sign of God's purpose for your life—even if it's not tennis or another sport—you're free to move ahead consistently and boldly. Then you feel good about yourself because you're a partner with God in the way He wants us all to be—living life abundantly."

 # My Rough Road to Obedience
Roger Staubach

Life took on extra excitement the day they began to build the new house next door to us. I was about seven, an only child, with a yearning for adventure. Aware of my fascination with the construction next door, Dad warned me, "You are not to go near that new house."

"Why?"

"Because you might get hurt."

Rebellious, I watched the house develop, floor by floor. The painters came and the house took on real luster. After the workers had mixed cement and carefully spread it on the front walk, the temptation to get a close look was too much. How could I get hurt when the house was almost finished!

Late in the afternoon after the workers had all gone home and while mother seemed to be quite involved in the basement, I crept stealthily into the forbidden territory and sat down beside the new cement walk. Carefully, I placed the palm of my right hand face down on the wet cement. It felt soft and cool. For a moment I studied the imprint of my hand on the walk. Then I placed my left hand on the cement.

"Hey, kid. Get outa there!"

Startled, I looked up. Striding toward me was a man whom I recognized as the supervisor. Like a startled fawn I bolted back into my house, the man in hot pursuit. From under the bed of my room I heard the doorbell ring, then voices in the living room.

That night I got it. First, a spanking from my father. Then the worst part—I was forbidden to use the playground across the street for two weeks.

Along with the punishment came an explanation that no family could function properly unless children obeyed their parents and that my disobedience had resulted in damage to property.

There were other times when I was disobedient and needed correction, but my parents, while firm, were always fair and loving about it. And it didn't take many punishments for me to see something very clearly: When I messed up, there was unhappiness in our home and I was miserable. When I obeyed the rules set down by my parents, there was harmony and contentment in our family.

Since my father made a rather unpredictable income as representative for a shoe firm, economy and discipline were essential in our home. Mother took a job when I was nine, so this meant shared duties all around.

And yet, while our rules were important, the more I accepted responsibility the more freedom and flexibility there was for me as I went from junior high on through high school.

Perhaps this is why the strict rules at the Naval Academy were so hard to take when I entered there in 1959. I could accept the need for order and routine, and even the ribbing plebes had to take from upperclassmen. But the time spent on keeping my shoes looking like mirrors and memorizing a lot of wordy regulations seemed so pointless.

My rebellion flared. Soon demerits were being posted in my record book, like points on the scoreboard during a high scoring basketball game. I collected over 100 demerits the first six months.

Furthermore, I was having academic problems as well, in metallurgy and mechanical drawing. It began to look as if my stay at Annapolis would be a very short one.

I suppose it was a combination of factors that helped straighten me out. Good advice from my parents. Plus the counsel of a young instructor who had graduated from the academy only a few years before.

"Roger, I know some of these rules seem like nonsense to you," he told me. "You and others think we're behind the times here at the academy. Changes will come—slowly. But the main purpose behind these regulations is to teach obedience. If military men don't learn to obey an order—whether they like it or not—we'll have chaos in our armed forces. In addition to that, I'm convinced that obedience is the key to the contented life."

When I did shape up, it worked out just as the instructor said. My grades went up, the demerits stopped accumulating, and one day I suddenly realized that I loved the place.

What then followed was a great football experience at Navy, but much more important than the awards and honors from football was learning something about that very elusive quality of leadership. To become a leader, I learned that you first have to be willing to accept authority.

But when I finished my stint in the Navy and joined the Dallas Cowboys in 1968, I found that once again, I still had something to learn about obedience. For what I loved so much about being quarterback for the Navy football team back in 1961-63 was the feeling that I was in command of an 11-man unit.

The quarterback of a football team directs the attack. He usually calls the plays in a huddle after getting advice and information from his teammates. The coach will occasionally send in instructions from the sidelines, but the quarterback is considered the commander of the offensive field unit.

But it didn't work that way in 1971 when Dallas won the professional football championship. At the beginning of the season, two quarterbacks were competing for the No. 1 position on the Dallas team—Craig Morton and me. Our coach, Tom Landry, alternated us for the first seven games.

One day he told me, "Roger, from now on you're my number one quarterback."

I was elated, of course, but soon found myself chafing at the conditions. As a quarterback of a team of outstanding players, I was only a partial leader. Coach Tom Landry called the plays, sending in his instructions during our huddles. I threw passes only when he said to, used the running plays he called. In an emergency situation, I could change a play on the line of scrimmage if I felt it was right—but I had better be right!

I'll admit it—a lot of the problem here was ego, my ego. With Coach Landry calling the plays, the implication was, of course, that quarterback Staubach was not good enough to know what plays to call.

When I was willing to go through a spiritual struggle to get self out of the way, the real facts emerged. I was darn lucky to be the No. 1 quarterback of one of the best teams in pro football. I *was* inexperienced and had a lot to learn about play calling in the pros. Coach Landry has one of the few "genius minds" when it comes to football strategy. We were winning, and I was playing well with our coach sending in the plays.

So again I faced up to the issue of obedience, suddenly aware of how it confronts you in different ways at different times in your life. What then happened was the same thing that happened in my home and at the Naval Academy. Once I learned to obey— harmony, fulfillment, victory.

The point still had to be rammed home in one more area of my life. This occurred at the birth of our fourth child. We were all greatly anticipating this big event—my wife Marianne and our three young daughters, Jennifer, Michele and Stephanie Marie.

But during the delivery something went wrong. The baby girl was stillborn.

I'll never forget that day at the cemetery when the tiny casket was lowered into the ground over which was the simple inscription "Baby Staubach." This was a real testing period of my life, for my father had passed away a year earlier.

As so many do in such personal crises, I asked the question, "Why, Lord?" Inside me once again were the stirrings of rebellion, this time against the Almighty who had such power over life and death.

It wasn't a long rebellion. Deep down I knew that strength came through my faith. When I prayed for understanding, I felt this sudden sense of peace and comfort. The Lord was Lord. He was with my daughter and my father. This world is not the end, but the beginning. If we believe in Him, there is the promise of eternal life.

Out of this acceptance has come gratitude for all He has given me: a strong body, clear mind, fine parents, a career doing what I like most to do—play football—a wife and three daughters whom I love very much. The old prophet Isaiah was right on target when he said, "If ye be willing and obedient, ye shall eat the good of the land" (Isaiah 1:19 KJV).

The Courage of One Who Kept on Going

Herschel Walker

(Written in 1982 while playing for the University of Georgia)

Football.

In Georgia, fall means football. It seems everyone is a football fan, that every team is someone's favorite. In Athens, 60,000 students, parents, alumni and just plain fans will pack the University of Georgia's Sanford Stadium, wearing red, and whooping and hollering for *their* Georgia Bulldogs.

I'm the Bulldogs' running back, and I can only hope that, win or lose, this season will not be like last.

It's not as if our 1981 record was bad—we won 10 games and lost only two. For the second straight year, we were Southeastern Conference Champions and ranked among the top 10 teams in the country. No, it wasn't the wins or losses at all that made last season so memorable. It was the way I nearly quit being a part of autumn in Georgia.

On the first day of football practice last fall, the Georgia Bulldogs were the toast of the state. We'd gone through the 1980 season undefeated and beaten Notre Dame in the Sugar Bowl, 17-10. Everywhere in Georgia, bumper stickers and T-shirts and Frisbees proclaimed the rallying cry of the previous season—"How 'bout them Dawgs?" We had won our last 13 games in a row, and hardly a fan could be found who didn't think we'd win another 12 in a row and the national championship again.

It had been a good year for me too. I had run for more yards than any freshman in the history of college football, and had finished as a runner-up for the prestigious Heisman Trophy, given each year to the nation's best college football player. I was just thankful that God had given me a gift—a strong body and a strong mind—and a chance to use that gift as best I could. Just being at the state university was special for me—it was an opportunity Mama and Daddy had only dreamed of for any of their seven children. But even as practice began, I could sense that that wasn't enough anymore. Last year was good, so this year would have to be better. For all our fans, nothing else would do.

I was in line to register for classes with the other students a few days before our first game when someone I didn't even know patted me on the back. "We can't lose this year!" he stated emphatically to his buddy as he turned to me. "Not with ol' Herschel out there for us." I suppose it was intended as a compliment, but the comment left me strangely uneasy. The responsibility that was being heaped on my shoulders scared me.

But out on the field, with a football tucked under my arm, I just tried to do what I did best—run toward the goal line. We beat Tennessee the first weekend of the season, 44-0, an outstanding team performance. The bell on top of the campus chapel rang out 14 times to celebrate our 14-game winning streak, now the longest in college football.

It rang 15 times the next week, after we struggled to a 27-13 win over California. I gained 167 yards rushing, but had fumbled once, just part of a team effort not quite up to par.

That's when the whispering started. It was isolated at first, a few inquiring people wondering if anything was wrong. Why hadn't I broken a long touchdown run yet? Was I worried that my play might jeopardize the winning streak? I was more confused, really. I had gained 328 yards in two wins. Was that so bad?

Coach Vince Dooley worked us hard as we prepared for the third game of the season against Clemson University. This year the game, one of the fiercest college rivalries in the South, would be in Clemson's Memorial Stadium, nicknamed "Death Valley" because of the difficulty opposing teams have winning there. Still, we were favored to win.

We won the coin toss, received the kickoff, and began moving the ball up the field. I picked up eight yards running around left end, another four slashing right. A pass play netted us another first down, and I carried twice more.

On second down, from the Clemson 13-yard line, I took a pitchout and headed left. Just as I was about to cut upfield toward the goal line, a Clemson lineman hit my arm. The ball squirted loose, and a pile of orange jerseys were immediately on top of it. I'd just fumbled away a good scoring chance.

I fumbled again in the second quarter to set up a Clemson field goal, but by that time our whole team had begun to unravel. Perhaps it was the noisy Clemson fans or just a bad day, but nine times that afternoon we lost the ball on fumbles or interceptions. We lost the game too, 13-3. The bell would not ring that night on the University of Georgia campus.

The locker room was somber as I shuffled in. Reporters surrounded us, probing for reasons for the loss. Herschel, what's wrong? Why aren't you playing like last year? Herschel, are you still happy at Georgia?

The Clemson defeat and the questions dogged me into the next week. No matter how hard I tried, I couldn't avoid it. One afternoon, as I walked to practice, two guys stopped me. "Hey, Herschel, how come you're not running like last year?" I shrugged, and mumbled something about doing my best and walked on. Though I had scored only one touchdown, compared to the five I'd scored after three games last season, I'd run for more yards. Yet, instead of "How 'bout them Dawgs?" everyone seemed to be asking, "What's wrong with Herschel?"

I walked on beneath the campus trees, thinking of the criticisms that had threaded their way in from every corner of Georgia, beginning to believe them myself. *Maybe I have lost it,* I thought. I'd even heard of bumper stickers that said, "Herschel Who?" The criticisms and doubts hurt, more than I cared to admit.

I dragged through practice halfheartedly, my mind focused more on what I would tell Coach Dooley than on how to run against South Carolina, our next opponent. I'd decided it might be easier to just quit, to forget the pressure and questions, the pain that came when your best effort wasn't good enough.

I also decided to wait until the next morning to say anything about quitting. As I dragged myself back to my room that night, I'd never felt so low and alone. Inside I flipped on a small light, and flopped down on my bed. "It's not fair," I said out loud. "Why is everybody on my case? Why can't I just be me?"

That's when I caught a glimpse of it out of the corner of my eye— the picture I had hanging over my bed, a picture of Jesus. It looked different this time, somehow. As I stared into Christ's face, I couldn't help but think about the stories of His life I'd learned back in Sunday school in Wrightsville, Georgia.

Maybe it was the recollection of those Bible stories that helped me realize what was different. In Jesus' face I saw for the first time an enormous courage. I saw a courage born in His 40-day struggle in the wilderness, and tested day in and day out by people who laughed at Him and threatened to arrest Him or stone Him. I saw the courage He showed on that final night in Gethsemane, when terrible agony forced huge drops of blood from His brow. In Jesus' face was the courage of One Who kept on going no matter what the hardship. There was no quitter in that picture.

For the longest time I just looked, drawing strength from the picture. And when I got to thinking again about why I needed that strength, I realized I'd found the example I needed to follow.

Whether the criticisms of me had been fair or not, it didn't matter, Herschel Walker would be no quitter, either.

I was the first one at practice the next day, attentively listening to the coaches' instructions. On the field, I ran with reckless abandon. No, the questions wouldn't stop, and the Clemson game would continue to be talked about. The fans were still expecting a lot from me. But I knew now how to cope with the pressure. By standing up to it, just as Jesus had, not running from it. I had a job to do!

That Saturday we defeated South Carolina, 24-0; I gained 176 yards and scored two touchdowns. We didn't lose again in the regular season; we won the conference title and were ranked second—behind Clemson.

Now, it's another football season at Georgia. Expectations are still high. And I'm determined to make it my best ever. I think I've got a good start because of what I learned last season: that no matter what job you do, there's Someone Who understands the pressure and responsibilities you face, Who's been through it Himself. Jesus will give you the strength and courage to keep going. Look for Him. And you'll see it, too.

Where Two or Three Are Gathered

Darrell Waltrip

My career as a race-car driver on the NASCAR circuit keeps me busy. Besides the demands of the racing itself, there are always business matters to arrange, sponsors to meet and a pit team to manage. And Sundays are generally my busiest days of all. Although my wife, Stevie, and I try to attend the church services that are held trackside in the morning, a few years ago I began to feel that the pressures of racing were crowding God out of my life.

One day I was having lunch with some friends and I confessed, "In my line of work, sometimes it's hard for me to keep my faith in proper perspective."

"You think it's easier for bankers?" my banker friend laughed. "Or for lawyers?" an attorney who joined us said. "Or for accountants?" an accountant friend of ours added. The fifth friend lunching with us that day was a part-time pastor, and he added sheepishly, "Or for ministers, for that matter?"

We could all remember times when our best intentions disappeared in a muddle of mundane matters. And yet we believed that our faith in God was the most important thing in our lives.

"We should find a way to support one another in this," someone said. And so we began gathering in the basement of our house in Franklin, Tennessee, each Tuesday morning for coffee, doughnuts, sausage biscuits and some honest talk about our faith. We turned to the Bible for guidance, offered one another advice and prayed together.

Then one of the guys invited a friend, another invited a neighbor. Word spread, and soon there were so many of us we couldn't fit in the basement. We moved to the patio on summer mornings. By wintertime we were meeting in our living room, almost 100 of us, some driving more than an hour to get there.

It's been three years since our first get-together, and by now our Tuesday gatherings have become a regular happening in my town. Jesus says, "For where two or three are gathered together in my name, there am I in the midst of them" (Matthew 18:20 RSV). If you're struggling with your faith the way I was, think about those words: *Where two or three are gathered*. Then act on them.